STO

ACPL ITEM
DISCARDED

36

HAWLEY, RICHARD A.
THINK ABOUT DRUGS AND
SOCIETY

YO-BVQ-647

DO NOT REMOVE
CARDS FROM POCKET

ALLEN COUNTY PUBLIC LIBRARY
FORT WAYNE, INDIANA 46802

You may return this book to any agency, branch,
or bookmobile of the Allen County Public Library.

DEMCO

THINK About
Drugs and Society

The THINK Series Editors: William N. Thorndike, Jr.
Ramsey R. Walker

Fact Checker: Susan Zesiger
Reading Consultants: Ann-Marie Longo, Paula Sable
Revised edition researched by Dorothy and
Thomas Hoobler

Jacket Designer: Georg Brewer
Text Designer: Joyce C. Weston
Copy editor: Victoria Haire
Photo Researcher: Diane Hamilton
Graph Designer: Jill Thompson
Text Illustrator: Jeff Danziger
Research Assistant: Caitlin Dixon

The editors would like to thank the many teachers, librarians,
and students who assisted in putting together the Think
series. It would be impossible to thank everybody; however,
we would especially like to thank the following people: John
Buckey, Betty Carter, Jim Davis, Mike Hartoonian, Tedd Levy,
David Mallery, Bill Polk, Mike Printz, Ellen Ramsey.

The THINK Series

THINK About
Drugs and Society

Responding to an Epidemic

Richard A. Hawley

Walker and Company
New York

Allen County Public Library
900 Webster Street
PO Box 2270
Fort Wayne, IN 46801-2270

Copyright © 1988, 1992 by Richard A. Hawley

All rights reserved. No part of this book may be
reproduced or transmitted in any form or by any means,
electronic or mechanical, including photocopying,
recording, or by any information storage and retrieval
system, without permission in writing from the Publisher.

This edition published in the United States of America
in 1992 by Walker Publishing Company, Inc.

Published simultaneously in Canada by Thomas Allen & Son
Canada, Limited, Markham, Ontario.

Library of Congress Cataloging-in-Publication Data
Hawley, Richard A.
    Think about drugs and society : responding to an
epidemic / Richard A. Hawley.—Rev. ed.
      p.   cm.—(The Think series)
    Includes bibliographical references and index.
    Summary: Describes the effects of drug abuse on the
individual and on society and discusses what can be done to
combat the problem.
    ISBN 0-8027-8114-4 (rein).—ISBN 0-8027-7366-4 (pbk.)
    1. Drug abuse—United States—Juvenile
literature.   2. Drug abuse—United States—Prevention—
Juvenile literature.   [1. Drug abuse.]   I. Title.   II. Series.
HV5809.5.H38   1992
362.29'0973—dc20   91-15730
                                                                CIP
                                                                AC

All photographs are printed with permission of the Library of
Congress. Figures on pages 9 and 67 copyright *Washington
Post:* reprinted by permission of the D.C. Public Library; Figure
on page 21 courtesy of the Toledo Museum of Art, Toledo,
Ohio; Figures on pages 23, 24, 28, 54, and 79 courtesy of the
Library of Congress; Figures on pages 35, 39, 44, 46, and 83
courtesy of the Drug Enforcement Administration (DEA).

Excerpt on pp. 107–108 from *From Chocolate to Morphine:
Understanding Mind-Active Drugs,* by Andrew Weil and
Winifred Rosen. Copyright 1983 by Andrew Weil and Winifred
Rosen. Reprinted by permission of Houghton Mifflin
Company.

Excerpt on pp. 108–110 from *Getting Tough on Gateway Drugs* by
Robert Dupont, M.D. Reprinted by permission of Robert
Dupont, M.D., and American Psychiatric Press.

Printed in the United States of America

10   9   8   7   6   5   4   3   2

CONTENTS

THINK About
Drugs and Society

INTRODUCTION

What's the problem?
What does a drug really do?
If drugs are so dangerous, why do people use them?
How is drug use changing society?
How did the drug epidemic get started?
Can the United States solve the problem?

The most serious problems facing modern peoples—crime, poverty, political oppression, warfare, and disease—have troubled civilization from its earliest recorded history. *Drug abuse,* on the other hand, seems to be a relatively new concern, one which has surfaced explosively in the twentieth century. While there is clear evidence that people used intoxicating chemicals before the present era, the extent to which mind-altering drugs are used and the variety of people who use them are new issues. Never before, for example, have large numbers of growing children used illegal drugs. Never before has a large population of women used drugs such as marijuana, which many researchers say will endanger the health of their future babies. Never before have so many people used drugs in open violation of the law. These developments, besides being new, are the source of serious medical, legal, and political problems.

WHAT IS THE DRUG PROBLEM?

Put in the simplest terms, the *drug problem* is that millions of people seek pleasurable feelings through the use of toxic, mind-altering chemicals. *Toxic* means "poisonous," and using toxic chemicals causes obvious losses in speech, thinking, movement, memory, and other important functions. But if the harmful effects of drug use are so well known, why does anyone use a drug in the first place?

Certain substances found naturally in plants and others created in laboratories can change the chemistry of the brain so that a person feels altered, different, "high." Sometimes the "high" produced can be so pleasurable that the drug user feels a strong desire to repeat the experience, despite the health and safety risk of doing so. People who continue their drug use run the risk of losing control over their decision to use, or not to use, drugs. When a person's craving for a drug is so great that he or she cannot resist using it, he or she is said to be *chemically dependent*. Chemically dependent people usually perform poorly at school or on the job. Their relationships with friends and family usually decline. Their health often becomes poor, and they run a high risk of early death by accident, illness, or drug overdose. When people become chemically dependent, they usually require the help of an organization like Alcoholics Anonymous, if not hospital care, in order to recover. The road to recovery can be very painful, and it is never easy. Discouragingly high numbers of people treated for drug problems relapse into drug use.

The national drug problem extends beyond the millions of people who become chemically dependent. Educators are concerned about drug-related declines in students' schoolwork and are currently working hard to correct the situation. Employers are worried about drug-related mistakes and inefficiency in the workplace. Law enforcement officials face increasing rates of drug-related crimes and highway accidents. Policymakers in government must respond to a growing, multibillion-dollar drug industry both within our national borders and beyond them.

Over sixty-five million Americans are estimated to have tried marijuana, an illegal drug in every state and an internationally regulated *controlled substance*. Over eleven million people are believed to be regular marijuana users. In addition, twenty-one million are estimated to have used cocaine, another drug prohibited by national and international law. When the number of users of other drugs is added to the number of underage users of such legal drugs as alcohol and tobacco, the number of drug-related law breakers appears staggeringly high. Some observers believe that such a large-scale rejection of drug laws undermines the effectiveness of all laws—and of law-abiding behavior itself. This increase in illegal activity of all kinds is a part of the drug problem.

WHAT IS MEANT BY *DRUG?*

Before exploring further how drug use affects society, some important terms should be defined. First, what is a drug? Americans live in a world of drugstores. Wonder drugs are praised for easing the symptoms of diseases. Obviously, there must be good drugs as well as bad ones.

But the notion of "good drugs" and "bad drugs" may be misleading. It is perhaps wiser to explore the difference between drugs and medicines. *Drug* may be defined as a substance taken for the pleasurable feelings it produces. By contrast, a *medicine* is defined as a substance taken to relieve the symptoms of an illness. Once they are defined, drugs and medicines are seen to have very different purposes. Drugs are used, in spite of their harmful side effects, to change the user's feelings. Users who get pleasurably high will want more of the drug that produced this feeling; thus, drug use reinforces itself.

By contrast, the goal of taking medicine usually is to stop taking it, to need it no longer. An exception is the chronically ill patient who takes medicine to relieve severe pain and discomfort. In some cases the same substance can be used as a medicine and abused as a drug. This does not mean that the toxic effects of that substance somehow disappear when it becomes "medicine." It means, rather, that the substance's healing effects are thought to outweigh its harmful ones.

Scientists have classified hundreds of different drugs. We cannot examine each of them, but it may be helpful to consider the general types of drugs and their effects. Drugs are classified by their effects on the brain and the rest of the nervous system:

1. *Depressants* are substances that slow down, or block, healthy nervous system activity. Depressants include alcohol, various chemicals whose vapors can be inhaled, opium and its by-products, and many chemicals produced in laboratories for medical purposes.
2. *Stimulants* are substances that chemically excite the nervous system by making it work harder and faster than it would normally. Cocaine, caffeine, nicotine, and various laboratory-produced chemicals such as amphetamine (or "speed") are stimulants.
3. *Hallucinogens* distort information coming into the brain and the brain's ability to interpret that infor-

mation. Hallucinogens appear to change the way things look, feel, smell, sound, and taste. They may also create in the user's mind images and events that are not really occurring. Hallucinogens are found in certain kinds of plants, such as cacti and mushrooms. Many others, such as LSD, are made in laboratories.

While different types of drugs affect people's brains, feelings, and behavior in different ways, drugs are alike in several ways:

1. Drugs change feelings and behavior by acting chemically on the brain.
2. Every known drug appears to damage the human system in one or more ways. All drugs, in other words, produce toxic effects and side effects; many of these effects are not consciously felt by the person taking them.
3. The use of any drug can result in chemical dependency.

In the past, scientists thought that only narcotic drugs like heroin caused chemical dependency (or addiction.). Over the past twenty years, however, there has been growing agreement that the use of any drug—cocaine, marijuana, tobacco, alcohol—can cause a life-threatening dependency. When we recognize the three points listed above, we see that drugs are more alike than they are different. The drug problem therefore includes the use of all drugs; it is not limited to the use of any particular drug or type of drug.

A final characteristic of drugs is that some are considered to be _threshold drugs_, that is, drugs that lead to the use of other drugs. Almost nobody who decides to try

a drug will begin with a powerful and reputedly dangerous substance such as heroin. But people who do
become dependent on heroin and other drugs tend to
start with substances that are more easily available and
that they believe to be less harmful. Cigarette smoking
and alcohol use by underage children are likely to
precede their decision to try a drug that is not legally
available, such as marijuana. People who are treated for
drug abuse almost always report that their drug use
began with underage drinking and smoking. Alcohol
and tobacco are a significant part of the drug problem,
not only because they often lead to more dangerous
drugs, but also because they cause more deaths than all
the other drugs combined.

A drug, then, is a substance taken for the pleasurable
feelings it produces. Medicine is a substance taken for
the relief from illness it provides. And we have seen that
there are different types of drugs: depressants, stimulants, and hallucinogens. However, despite the differences, drugs are more similar than they are different:
They all change feelings and behavior; they all damage
the human system in one or more ways, and they all
can result in chemical dependency. The drug problem
includes all drugs, "pot" (marijuana) and alcohol just as
much as cocaine and heroin, and it includes all people,
those who take drugs as well as the rest of society.

WHY IS THERE A DRUG-ABUSE EPIDEMIC NOW?

The drug epidemic in the United States appears to have
a clear beginning. Before 1964, drug abuse—especially
among children—was not a great national concern. It
prompted no television specials. Medical, legal, and
educational journals devoted their pages to other issues.

After 1964, however, the picture quickly changed. Television and printed news were full of references to a new "youth movement," "youth culture," or "counterculture."

The image of young people in the sixties was both rebellious and free-spirited. Both sexes wore their hair longer, and clothes were often worn more as "costumes" than as uniforms. Extremely popular varieties of rock music—from such new groups as the Beatles and the Rolling Stones—further united the youth movement.

Almost from its beginning, the new youth culture took to the casual or "recreational" use of drugs. This kind of behavior had previously been limited, with few exceptions, to the urban poor, to criminals, and to various nonconformists. This willingness to use illegal drugs became what scientists call an epidemic. *Epidemic* is the rapid spread of any occurrence, whether a disease, a behavior, or even a fashion. In the United States the drug epidemic began on college campuses and spread within a few years to the school-age population. The use patterns of marijuana—a threshold drug—show how quickly the epidemic progressed. Before 1964 it was estimated that no more than 4 percent of the entire population had tried marijuana. By 1975 the percentage of high school seniors who had used marijuana was over 40 percent. By 1980, 60 percent of the high school students surveyed nationally indicated that they had tried the drug. But this was the peak of marijuana drug use among young people. Throughout the 1980s, fewer of America's teenagers tried marijuana. By 1989, the percentage of high school students who had used marijuana had dropped to 43.7 percent, a significant decline. Still, tens of millions of people nationwide have used marijuana, a complicated substance containing many toxic chemicals—a drug that is illegal to produce, distribute, and (in most states) to possess.

Why has this interest in marijuana persisted? One explanation is that for almost a decade, beginning in the middle 1960s, the bulk of the population was young. For several of those years there were more Americans under twenty-five than there were over that age. This population "bulge" was also the most affluent and mobile generation in history. Millions of these young people resided together on college campuses, with very little adult supervision to restrict them. The youth culture's opposition to the Vietnam War (1964–73) and to the military draft, and their efforts to promote minority rights, further divided them from the adult "establishment." One of the issues over which the generations battled was the "right" to use drugs.

By the middle 1960s, illegal drug use was "out of the closet." Popular music and films made references to taking drugs, and several famous performers flaunted their own use of drugs. The refrain of a popular Beatles song was "I get high with a little help from my friends." The overall image of drug taking, at least among young people, became more favorable. Society's traditional opposition to drug use softened as law enforcement officials found it difficult to enforce laws prohibiting the use and possession of small amounts of certain drugs. As the epidemic gained momentum, organized crime both in the United States and abroad moved quickly to meet the new and profitable demand for drugs.

The political issues, hairstyles, and musical tastes of the 1960s have passed on, but drug use has taken

This photo, taken in 1971, shows an anti-Vietnam demonstration in Washington, D.C.

hold. Throughout the 1970s, illegal drug use increased. A turning point came in the 1980s as the word got around that drug use was not risk-free. By the end of the decade the likelihood of a high school or college student actively using illicit drugs was less than it had been in 1980. According to the National Institute on Drug Abuse, some 51 percent of high school seniors and 56 percent of college students have tried illicit drugs at least once.

Still, these figures are too high for the nation's health. Hundreds of thousands of school-age children have become chemically dependent. While a direct link is difficult to prove, higher rates of drug use among the young have contributed to other problems in society since the drug epidemic began, including rising crime rates, a drop in the scores on national aptitude tests, and a rise in the number of unwanted teenage pregnancies. Concern over alcohol and drug-related highway accidents has reached such a pitch that federal highway funds are now withheld from any state that does not raise its drinking age to twenty-one.

IS WIDESPREAD DRUG USE CONTROLLABLE?

Since drugs act so immediately and so powerfully to change the way people feel and behave, it is not surprising that if large numbers of people are allowed

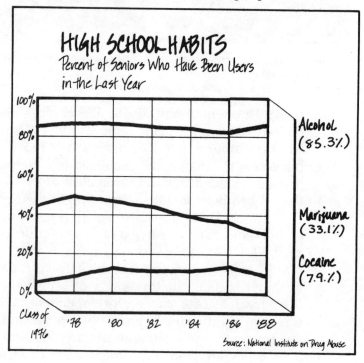

HIGH SCHOOL HABITS
Percent of Seniors Who Have Been Users in the Last Year

Alcohol (85.3%)

Marijuana (33.1%)

Cocaine (7.9%)

Source: National Institute on Drug Abuse

to use drugs, unmanageable social problems usually follow. Attempts to control drug use will vary with a society's political system, traditions, and religious beliefs. After World War I, the people of the United States expressed a widely felt frustration with alcohol abuse. A grass-roots movement finally became national law when the Constitution was amended to prohibit "the manufacture, sale, or transportation" of all alcoholic beverages. Two-thirds of Congress voted for Prohibition, and thirty-six states ratified the amendment. But Prohibition (1919–33) did not "take" in the United States. The law was widely violated and resented as an unreasonable restriction of personal freedom. Some scholars have suggested that national drinking habits were too deeply rooted to be changed overnight by the mere passage of a law.

Some nations have met with better success than the United States in their efforts to crack down on drug problems. Between 1951 and 1953, the People's Republic of China successfully wiped out what had been a 300-year pattern of opium use. Both Japan and Sweden successfully reversed the epidemic use of stimulant drugs. The Islamic holy scripture, the Koran, forbids the use of alcohol, and the prohibition is largely successful in Moslem nations. But while Moslem countries have also made strict laws against the use of cannabis (the plant that produces marijuana and hashish), there is no religious rule against it. As a result, cannabis abuse has been a documented problem in the Moslem world for 1,000 years.

So what is the answer? Strict government or religious prohibition? In an "open society" like the United States, what kind of consensus (popular agreement) would be necessary in order to prohibit drug use effectively? Should reformers seek to eliminate drug supply by cracking down on growers, smugglers, and dealers? Or should they work to eliminate demand, by educating citizens, especially children, about the dangers of drug use? Should drug education be aimed more at threshold substances such as tobacco and alcohol, or at deadly street killers such as "crack" (refined cocaine)? Since drug use has progressed so far already, would government regulation of drugs work better than prohibition?

While drug use worldwide is an increasingly prominent issue, no clearly effective solutions to the problem have yet been devised. Perhaps part of the difficulty lies in the very nature of drug taking. Drugs change the way people feel and behave. In addition, drugs affect the user's ability to judge the effects of drug use. A drunken man does not know he is driving less effectively. The chronic marijuana smoker who "doesn't care" about schoolwork or family relationships anymore is not aware that a drug has made him unable to care. The cocaine user does not want to believe that cocaine is emptying her bank account and radically changing her life.

Societies with large populations already destructively involved in the use of drugs have an especially difficult problem to resolve. A failure to resolve it could result in that society's rapid decline. Drug use has increased significantly over the past two decades. It endangers the health of individuals and society. How individuals, communities, schools, or governments respond to this problem is a complex and difficult issue, but one that can be addressed. In this book, we will look first at the history of three widely used drugs: alcohol, marijuana, and cocaine.

Equipped with this historical background, we can explore various drug-related issues. You can then decide what you think about drugs and society.

REVIEW QUESTIONS

1. In what ways is drug abuse a "new" problem?
2. How widespread is the current drug problem in the United States? Who is primarily affected by it?
3. Besides endangering health, how do drugs affect society?
4. What are the differences between using a drug and using a medicine?
5. In what ways do different classes of drugs affect the human system? In what ways are all drugs alike?
6. When did epidemic drug use begin in this century? Why do you think drug use increased so quickly in the 1960s?

1 Historical Background

What's new about drug use—and what isn't?
Alcohol: A holy sacrament? Social beverage? Killer drug?
Marijuana: Where has it been all this time?
What happens to marijuana-using societies in the long run?
Cocaine: Will it prove to be the deadliest pleasure?
Why does the use of these drugs continue?

An American soldier returning home from World War II probably could not have imagined that within his lifetime drug abuse would become a major national problem. He would not have imagined a multibillion-dollar traffic in illegal drugs. Nor could he have imagined the economies of whole states in the United States being dominated by the drug trade. He would not have imagined distinguished lawyers, business leaders, and star athletes taking—and occasionally dying from the use of—illegal drugs. Nor could he have imagined millions of school-age children using drugs. Yet these very developments would become reality for his children and his grandchildren.

While a drug problem of this scale is a very recent development in the United States, drug use itself goes far back in human history. Perhaps looking at the way people lived with, and without, drugs in the past may shed some light on the current situation in the United States.

As long ago as 1000 B.C., ancient Egyptian wall paintings show the elite classes socializing over wine and beer. Egyptian documents include many references to drunkenness, including a warning to schoolboys to stay away from beer halls. At the same time, across the Atlantic Ocean, the Indians of ancient Mexico practiced rituals in which parts of the peyote (pay-oh-tee) cactus were eaten in order to reach a state of religious trance. Many mind-altering substances, including opium and cannabis, were once believed to have healing properties, but later became drugs of abuse. This chapter will explore the history of three widely used drugs: alcohol, marijuana, and cocaine. At the end of the chapter we will explore some reasons why the use of these drugs persists. Perhaps this historical background will shed some light on how we can respond to the drug epidemic today.

A BRIEF HISTORY OF THREE INTOXICATING DRUGS

Alcohol

Alcoholic beverages have been consumed by peoples all over the world for thousands of years. No one knows who first discovered alcohol, nor does its use appear to have begun in any particular region. Many ancient peoples seem to have come up with alcohol on their own.

For most of recorded history, alcohol (full scientific

name: ethyl alcohol) was consumed in the form of wine (fermented grape juice) or beer (fermented cereal broth). In the classical civilizations of Greece and Rome (c. 500 B.C.–A.D. 500) the drinking of beer and wine was a standard feature of everyday life. Both Jews and Christians accepted fermented beverages as part of God's gift of creation. Wine is used as a medicine, as a religious symbol, and as a social beverage in both the Old and New Testaments of the Judeo-Christian Bible. In the New Testament, Jesus, himself, produces some especially good wine at a wedding celebration.

In some parts of the world, drinking alcohol was not an accepted practice. The founding prophet of Islam, Muhammad (A.D. 570–632), took offense at the drinking he saw around him in the Near East. In the sacred book that he dictated, the Koran, the consumption of alcohol is forbidden on Earth.

In the late Middle Ages (about A.D. 1200), Europeans learned to make a form of alcohol that was purer and more potent than beer or wine. The new method, *distillation*, involved boiling fermented juices, collecting the alcoholic vapors as they rose into tubes, then condensing the vapors into liquid. This more concentrated form of alcohol is called *distilled spirits*. Gin, vodka, rum, tequila, brandy, and various kinds of whiskey (scotch, rye, bourbon, Canadian) are all distilled spirits. They usually contain between 40 and 50 percent alcohol. The *proof* of distilled alcohol is twice the amount of its alcohol percentage. In other words, a bottle of gin with 40 percent alcohol in it is called 80 proof. By comparison, the alcohol content of most beers is about 5 percent, and that of wines is normally 10–14 percent.

Because spirits contain so much more alcohol than beer and wine, they are usually taken in smaller amounts. Sometimes people become confused and think that because the percentage of alcohol in beer is lower than it is in other kinds of alcoholic beverages, they are therefore drinking less total alcohol than they would be if they were drinking wine or spirits. The fact is that a shot glass of whiskey, a can of beer, and a typical glass of wine all contain about the same amount of alcohol: one ounce. The ounce will have the same effect on the drinker, regardless of what kind of beverage it comes from.

The European colonists brought their taste for alcoholic beverages with them to North America. Beer and wine were drunk with meals and during celebrations. Even the Puritans, who held very strict views against laziness, immodest dress, wastefulness, and luxury, accepted fermented drinks as a "good creature of God." Distilled spirits also found a place in the New World. The colonial molasses trade led to the distilling of rum, and the Scotch-Irish settlers brought their "secret method" of distilling whiskey with them across the Atlantic in the early 1700s.

Drunkenness, however, was frequently a problem. It was especially so on the western frontier of the colonies, where government regulation and normal social restraints were not strongly felt. In fact, throughout American history, the Frontier, as it expanded westward to the Pacific, has been the scene of legendary hard-drinking and lawlessness.

The settlers' drinking habits in many ways clashed with those of the native Americans they encountered. Native Americans had for centuries consumed fermented beverages of their own, mainly winelike

Alcohol and the problems it causes for those that abuse it have existed from classical times through the founding of the United States and continue to exist today.

drinks made from nuts and corn. However, distilled spirits—"hard liquor"—were new to them. Since the European settlement of North America, the rate of alcohol problems among Native Americans has increased to tragically high levels.

As we have seen, the Europeans who settled in North America were not opposed to drinking. Neither the British crown nor the newly independent colonies were interested in stopping or changing people's drinking habits. After the new United States government was formed, however, it insisted on the right to regulate and to tax the production and sale of alcohol.

In 1794 a very unpopular federal tax on whiskey caused an angry rebellion among the settlers of western Pennsylvania. President George Washington's government was brand new, and it needed money.

The Scotch-Irish settlers in western Pennsylvania were active distillers of whiskey. In fact, because they had more whiskey than money, they used to exchange gallons of liquor for currency. Understandably, these Pennsylvanians resented the tax, and they began tarring and feathering the federal agents who came to enforce the new tax law. Thus began what historians call the Whiskey Rebellion. In response, President Washington sent an army of 13,000 troops, who marched to the scene of the rebellion and quickly stopped it. The federal government has maintained its right to tax and to regulate drinking ever since.

As the young nation matured and expanded westward, there was much concern over the destructive effects of drinking. This concern was especially evident in the South and on the Frontier, where visitors and settlers found drunkenness and violence to a discouraging degree. By the 1830s the *temperance (antidrink) movement* was well under way in the United States.

Through the beginning of this century, heavy drinking—what would today be called alcoholism—was associated far more with men than with women. Men typically had more money at their disposal and moved about more freely. Men could socialize and drink in clubs, lounges, and saloons without losing respectability; women typically could not. But if men actually drank more, women, especially wives, may have been the ones who suffered most. For when the breadwinner spent his pay on a drinking binge, his wife and family had to do without. There were no public agencies or "hotlines" to shelter and support wives and children battered by drunken men.

This painting by John Lewis Krimmel depicts a tavern in Ohio in the early 1800s.

When an alcoholic man abandoned his family, his wife would not be likely to find employment. Nor would she be given credit at banks and stores. In fact, she stood a poor chance of being allowed to open a bank account of her own. Nor, until 1920, could she express her dissatisfaction about such things through the ballot box. Increasingly, however, women began to speak up about drinking and its effects on their welfare.

In 1874 a remarkable woman named Frances E. Willard succeeded in organizing a national Women's

Christian Temperance Union (WCTU). *Temperance* means "moderation" or "restraint," yet most women who joined the WCTU felt that abstinence (no use) was the correct approach to alcohol. During the same period, one passionate woman from Kansas, Carry A. Nation, took a more dramatic approach to the problem. Infuriated by her first husband's death from alcoholism, she took to entering saloons and smashing them up with a hatchet.

Women were not alone in rising to oppose the use of alcohol. Thousands of members of the American Temperance Society, which included children's clubs, had been active since 1826. A new political party, the National Prohibition party, was formed in 1869, and an influential Anti-Saloon League was organized in 1893. Many of the original temperance-society members hoped for moderation in the use of alcohol. But as the century wore on, opinion changed. Drunkenness continued to be a public nuisance, a brutal reality in many households, and a danger to economic productivity. More and more people came to

Heavy drinking on the Frontier gave rise to antialcohol sentiment.

believe that total abstinence from alcohol (also called *teetotalism*) was the only solution.

In 1846 the state of Maine passed a law prohibiting the sale and manufacture of alcoholic beverages. Within a few years, twelve other states and western territories would do the same. The laws were sometimes repealed and ignored. However, these early expressions of frustration with alcohol abuse continued and eventually led to passage of the Eighteenth Amendment, which prohibited producing and selling alcohol nationwide.

The Eighteenth Amendment was ratified in 1919. The same year, Congress passed the Volstead Act, which provided the money and the means to enforce

This lithograph from 1894 cleverly shows the problems that arose from alcohol abuse and reflects the rise in antialcohol sentiment at the turn of the century.

this amendment. It took some time before the enforcement machinery was ready to operate, but Prohibition officially went into effect in January 1920. Prohibition lasted for thirteen years before it was repealed, but it was never effective. Its critics claimed that it was hopeless to ban what so many people obviously wanted. Others felt that Prohibition violated basic personal liberty. A prominent American historian, Thomas A. Bailey, wrote, "You can't legislate against a thirst." One might argue, however, that few people turn to alcohol merely to quench their thirst.

With hindsight it is clear that the national prohibition policy was not designed very well. There were not nearly enough federal officials to enforce the new laws. Smuggling (*bootlegging*) and illegal distilling

This photo, taken in 1923, shows cases of illegally made beer being destroyed in Washington, D.C., during Prohibition.

(*moonshining*) became widespread. Illegal bars and clubs called speakeasies appeared in major cities. The great popular demand for illegal alcohol played into the hands of organized crime, which expanded greatly during Prohibition. While it was in effect, Prohibition did sharply decrease the overall level of alcohol consumption, especially among poorer people who had no spare income for bootleggers' fees or expensive evenings at a speakeasy. By 1933 a majority of drinkers and nondrinkers alike believed that Prohibition was unfair and ineffective. It took only ten months for the necessary thirty-six states to pass the Twenty-First Amendment, which repealed Prohibition.

Prohibition did not solve the country's drinking problem, but repealing Prohibition has not solved it either. Today in the United States about seven adults out of ten drink alcohol socially, approximately 110 million people in all. More than ten million of them

During Prohibition, some people set up their own stills to produce alcohol. Most of the illegally made alcohol was made and sold by organized-crime groups.

are estimated to be problem drinkers. Alcohol-related accidents are the number-one cause of violent death in the United States. Drunk drivers are involved in nearly 40 percent of all highway deaths; 17,580 people died in such accidents in 1989. Other studies show that a very high percentage of sex offenses and other violent crimes are committed while the offender is under the influence of alcohol.

Heavy drinking also contributes to a number of serious and fatal illnesses, including heart disease, cirrhosis of the liver, various digestive-tract cancers, and organic diseases of the brain. Heavy alcohol consumption by pregnant women has been shown to harm the developing fetus (fetal alcohol syndrome). Alcohol also reacts chemically with other drugs and medicines to produce extremely toxic and even fatal effects.

So the alcohol problem in the United States is far from solved. No aspect of the problem is more serious than the illegal use of alcohol by growing children. Children who drink intoxicating beverages before their bodies are fully developed run the risk of never realizing their full, healthy potential as learners, athletes, performers, and partners in satisfying relationships. Every developing child who uses alcohol takes this risk. Children of alcoholics run an even greater risk. They are *twice* as likely to become alcoholics as are children of parents who are not alcoholics. There are at present about thirty million children of alcoholics in the United States—a number equal to the population of the state of California.

The national population is growing, and the rate of alcohol use is growing with it. It is clear that even more lives, more health, and more productivity will be lost in the years ahead, unless Americans somehow change their approach to alcohol. The current national strategies to fight alcohol problems will be discussed in Chapter 4.

Cannabis

Cannabis, or hemp, is the plant from which the drug marijuana is made. The use of cannabis has been traced back 4,000 years to ancient China. It was originally used as an all-purpose medicine, but there is no record of the Chinese using it as a pleasure-producing drug.

The peoples of ancient India also investigated the uses of cannabis, probably as a result of their trade with China. In some regions of India, Hindu priests drank cannabis teas as a part of religious rituals. Over the centuries cannabis use spread to the common people of India, who were probably the first to smoke it instead of eating or drinking it. From India, cannabis use spread throughout Asia.

In spite of its ancient origins, cannabis has only been studied closely by scientists for about twenty years. Important studies are still in progress. One reason cannabis has been difficult to study is that the substance is very complex. Marijuana, for instance, is made up of dried parts of the cannabis plant, including leaves, flowers, resins, and stems. Cannabis contains more than 420 different chemical substances. The molecules found only in cannabis and in no other plant are called cannabinoids. Some of the cannabinoids are *psychoactive,* which means that they chemically alter brain functions. The most psychoactive chemical in marijuana is *delta-9 THC,* and it is most responsible for making users high. Israeli scientists

A man smoking marijuana.

identified delta-9 THC for the first time in 1965, and since then the scientific understanding of how the drug works has advanced greatly.

Cannabis's power to intoxicate the user depends on how much THC it contains. Hemp plants growing wild in the plains of North America may contain only a fraction of a percent of THC. Mexican marijuana contains 1 percent THC; Asian marijuana, 2–4 percent; Jamaican, 4–8 percent. A very potent form of marijuana called sinsemilla, grown in California, contains 10–14 percent THC. Some forms of marijuana, then, are twice, ten times, even a hundred times more potent than others. At higher THC levels, marijuana is not a "mild" or "soft" drug, but rather a powerful one that can cause hallucinations, as well as a number of other dramatic changes such as loss of time sense, feelings of extreme fear, irregular heart-beat, and long-term, chronic memory loss.

Cannabis preparations are called by different names in different places. Marijuana is the most common name for cannabis in the United States, Canada, and Mexico. Street names include pot, weed, grass, reefer, and jay. In some regions the resins secreted by the cannabis flowers are concentrated into little balls to form hashish. Like ordinary marijuana, hashish is either smoked or eaten, but its THC content is very high, about 10 percent. More potent still is hashish oil, a dark liquid made by treating marijuana with a chemical solvent. The THC content of hashish oil may be as high as 60 percent.

Marijuana stays in the body much longer than alcohol and most other drugs do. An ounce of alcohol, for example, is broken down by enzymes in the liver and metabolized in an hour or two. Marijuana's THC, however, does not break down quickly in the human system. The THC is stored in the fatty parts of brain cells and of other cells all over the human body. THC blocks the healthy flow of fluids in and out of cells, and in time causes those cells to deteriorate. Half the THC from a single marijuana cigarette may remain in the body a week after it is smoked. Some of it is still detectable forty days after its use. The toxic effects of marijuana therefore continue long after the hour or so during which a user feels "high." Since marijuana appears to damage the cells and tissues that absorb it, its long storage period is a serious medical concern.

Through most of recorded history, the use of cannabis has been confined to certain groups within society: some priests, who used it only in religious

Research on marijuana has been active for over twenty years.

ceremonies; many laborers who performed simple and repetitive tasks (such as sugar cane harvesters in Jamaica); and criminals. Before this century, cannabis had rarely been used widely throughout a society. Some historians believe one exception might have occurred in the thirteenth century in Egypt. According to these historians, Egyptians of all classes began using hashish under the reign of the Mameluk kings (A.D. 1250–1517). This increased use of cannabis coincided with a sharp economic and social decline, ending in the total domination of Egypt by the Turks. Some experts believe that the increase in drug use contributed to Egypt's decline.

In the Arab world, cannabis use has been traditionally limited to men. Only in the twentieth century, in Western Europe and the United States, have large numbers of women begun to use cannabis.

In the United States, cannabis was not used as a pleasure-producing drug until relatively recently. Beginning in colonial days, some farmers harvested cannabis (hemp) for its fiber value. George Washington's own farm produced an annual crop of hemp for rope making. Beginning in the middle of the last century, very small amounts of cannabis were used in patent medicines. These medicines were used for such varied symptoms as relief of menstrual cramps, sore tonsils, and lockjaw. The amount of cannabis in the medicines were so small that users were unlikely to feel any intoxicating effects.

In the mid-1850s, a young man in Poughkeepsie, New York, named Fitz Hugh Ludlow read an account about opium use and decided to seek a similar experience for himself. From a pharmacist friend he was given a bottle of medicine called Tilden's Extract of

Cannabis Indica (*Indica* meant that it was imported from India) and proceeded to take large doses over the course of several days. Ludlow reported experiencing both pleasant and unpleasant hallucinations, as well as some disturbing heart symptoms. He continued to use cannabis but was finally worried enough about its effects on his health that, with the help of a doctor, he stopped using it. Ludlow died at age thirty-four, from what doctors at the time believed to be tuberculosis. However, it is possible his health was weakened by his drug experiments, leaving him more vulnerable to deadly disease.

Even though Ludlow wrote a book about his experiences, his example seemed to attract no immediate followers. Cannabis made little impact on American life until about 1910, when marijuana was brought in to the South by Mexican migrants. Widespread use was reported among poor black and Mexican farm workers, and New Orleans emerged as the hub of marijuana traffic. By 1926, the *New Orleans Morning Tribune* would be denouncing "The Marijuana Menace." Within a few years, as use of marijuana spread, other cities would voice similar concerns.

By the 1930s marijuana was still mainly limited to the very poor, to criminals, and to certain musicians and artists. Although the estimated number of users was thought to be small, government officials feared that an epidemic might develop. The fears most often expressed about marijuana use were that it led to increased crime rates and addiction to other drugs, such as heroin.

The uneasy response to marijuana use in the United States took the form of various new antimarijuana laws, some at the national level, others at the state and local level. In 1937 Congress passed the Marijuana Tax Act, which prohibited the sale, distribution, and possession of cannabis.

Worldwide concern about the harmful effects of cannabis was growing faster than it was in the United States. Nations of the Near East, and Egypt especially, wanted powerful Western countries like the United States to help control what they called "brown drugs" (drugs made from cannabis) and not just "white drugs" (those made from the opium poppy, such as heroin).

In 1961 the United Nations adopted a sweeping policy to control "narcotic and stupefying drugs." This resolution, called the Single Convention on Narcotic Drugs (see Appendix), was agreed upon by seventy-four participating nations. The Single Convention includes cannabis among the most dangerous drugs of abuse. The Single Convention requires nations to cooperate in banning the production and distribution of cannabis, except for closely supervised medical purposes.

The United States' agreement with the Single Convention was soon overshadowed by the epidemic use of marijuana that began with the 1960s youth movement. Over the past three decades, cannabis use has risen to the point that a majority of high school students report that they have used marijuana at least once. Nationwide there are an estimated twenty-five million regular users. With the rise in the number of users, marijuana has become big business. Illegal cultivation of marijuana has become a significant rival to the growing of fruits and vegetables in the state of California. Florida is also a major point of entry for illegal drugs.

As we have seen, marijuana use and the marijuana business grew tremendously before scientists, doctors, and educators rose up to oppose it. One reason for this slow response was that very little was known scientifically about cannabis. THC was not discovered until 1965, and a standard grade of marijuana for use in tests would not be developed until several years afterward. Without this standard grade (27 percent THC) marijuana for use in experiments, the validity of marijuana research could easily be challenged and denied. Another reason was that few parents and teachers of the new generation of marijuana users had enough experience with marijuana to respond to it confidently. Some parents were angry about youthful marijuana use. Others tried to accept it, and still others were honestly confused.

Another reason that marijuana was not more strongly opposed was that, in the 1960s, smoking pot was seen as part of a youthful life-style, not as a dangerous threat to health. The young people who first defied marijuana laws also tried out new tastes in dress and music. Many of them were politically active. In general, the movement symbolized by the free-spirited "hippie" expressed a desire for a simpler, more personal, less routine world. "Make love, not war" and "If it feels good, do it!" were two prominent slogans of the day. Millions of schoolchildren and young adults found that getting high on marijuana felt good, so they did it.

Now, twenty-five years later, the styles and political concerns of the 1960s have been replaced by current ones. The exception is drug use, including marijuana use. Drug use seems to have taken hold. New drugs (called "designer drugs") make the scene each year, and new forms of older drugs (such as "crack") gain popularity. No drugs of abuse have disappeared from the scene, however.

The use of marijuana is no longer considered a fad or a trend. Nor is it considered harmless or only a mild intoxicant. As marijuana research continues, the alarm over the drug's threat to health grows with it.

Effects on the brain. It was mentioned earlier that cannabis drugs store themselves in the body's fat tissue. This is important from a health standpoint, because every cell in the human body contains fat. The brain and its connecting nerves are rich in fat, as are the other vital organs. Research carried out by Doctor Robert Heath in laboratories at Tulane University revealed brain damage in rhesus monkeys that were exposed to cannabis smoke over a period of several months. Brain cells of monkeys that were exposed to the equivalent of two to three marijuana

Haight-Ashbury is the section of San Francisco where the hippie life-style flourished in the sixties.

cigarettes per day were found to be significantly damaged. Nervous-system damage is especially serious, because nerve cells do not grow back or repair themselves once they are destroyed; lost brain cells are lost forever.

Effects on the lungs. Most cannabis users smoke the drug in cigarettes or pipes. Marijuana smoke irritates the mouth, throat, and lungs in much the same manner that tobacco smoke does. Like tobacco, marijuana contains tar and other chemicals that block healthy lung activity. In fact, research shows that one marijuana cigarette irritates the lungs as much as twenty tobacco cigarettes (one pack). Research tests in Switzerland, performed on lung tissue, indicate that cannabis can change healthy cells into cancerous, tumor-producing ones. Cannabis smoke also contributes to chronic lung diseases such as bronchitis and emphysema. Marijuana smokers generally inhale the smoke deeply and hold it in the lungs for several seconds, thereby maximizing its harmful effects on healthy lung tissue.

Effects on reproduction. Cannabis has a number of important effects on reproductive health. In males, cannabis decreases the amount of testosterone (the main male sex hormone) that the body produces. Cannabis has also been found to decrease the number of sperm cells that the body produces, while increasing the number of abnormal sperm cells. Female hormones are also affected; cannabis causes irregularities in the menstrual cycle. THC and other chemicals in cannabis pass from a pregnant woman's bloodstream into the system of her developing baby.

There have been no systematic studies of the effects of cannabis on normal and abnormal human births, but monkeys whose mothers have been exposed to cannabis in laboratory tests tend to be undersized and hyperactive.

Mice who are given cannabis produce a significantly higher percentage of abnormal offspring than do mice who are not given the drug. There is growing scientific agreement that cannabis poses an even greater danger to developing fetuses than alcohol and tobacco do.

Marijuana has been used since ancient times. Its use and its users, however, have changed significantly. Traditionally, it was used by a limited part of the population. Its use now is far more widespread. It is used by men and women from all backgrounds and segments of society. Recent evidence shows the dangerous effects of marijuana use to the brain, heart, lungs and to sexual potency. This evidence makes it necessary for us to think closely about our response to marijuana use.

Cocaine

Like alcohol and cannabis, the South American coca plant has been used as a drug since ancient times. Coca leaves have been found in Peruvian grave sites dating back to 2500 B.C. The Inca civilization, which reached its height about A.D. 1000, was also familiar with mind-altering coca preparations. At first, coca use seems to have been limited to Inca priests who used it to reach trancelike states. Later, coca leaves were given to mine workers and field hands to chew. Both the Inca rulers and the Spanish conquerors later found that Incan peasants worked harder in the often harsh climate of the Andes high country (and also required less food) if they chewed a "cud" of coca leaves as they worked. This practice has continued among Andes laborers even today, principally among men. The life expectancy of these workers was about thirty years at the time of Pizarro's conquest of the Incas in A.D. 1531, and it is about the same today.

Cocaine is purified by treating the leaves with kerosene, sulfuric acid, and other chemicals. This treatment produces what is called *coca base,* which is about 80 percent pure cocaine. The coca base is further treated with hydrochloric acid to produce a white, powdery salt which is 90–100 percent pure cocaine. Cocaine dealers usually dilute, or "cut," the pure cocaine to between a quarter and an eighth of its strength. Some of the substances added to street cocaine themselves are mind-altering drugs. Simple sugars and powders are also added for bulk.

Pure cocaine was first produced in a laboratory by a German scientist in 1859. European doctors at that

A coca field.

time were looking for effective anesthetics (chemical pain-blockers), and many of them eagerly took up the experimental use of cocaine. At first, some of the physicians who injected themselves with a cocaine solution believed that they had found a new wonder drug. A young ophthamologist named Koller used it successfully with patients who were undergoing eye surgery. Sigmund Freud (1856–1935), the father of modern psychiatry, tried cocaine himself and prescribed it to his wife, friends, and patients as a remedy for depression and nervous disorders.

Soon after he began his experiments, however, Freud began noting physical and mental breakdowns among cocaine-using patients. Three years after he had first used cocaine, Freud denounced it as dangerous and harmful.

Toward the end of the last century a prominent young surgeon at Johns Hopkins Hospital became dependent on the cocaine he had been prescribing for patients. Unable to work in his dependent condi-

Cocaine hydrochloride.

tion, he finally had to be hospitalized and afterward was able to function only with the aid of another drug, morphine.

While the medical profession was still learning about cocaine, the drug's stimulating "feel-good" effects made it a popular addition to medicines sold over the counter. In the late 1800s a coca wine called Vin Mariani was marketed all over Europe as a reliever of malaria, influenza, and many other illnesses. Cocaine-containing medicines in all forms—tablets, powders, liquids, ointments—were advertised as cures for practically every ailment.

In 1886 a pharmacist in Atlanta patented a medicine that combined coca leaves, a small amount of pure cocaine, and flavoring from the Kola nut. At first this mixture, a syrup, was sold to relieve headaches and mental irritation. In 1891 the formula was purchased by another Atlanta pharmacist and the Coca Cola Company was born.

The new carbonated beverage was sold as a light tonic in drugstores before the (very small amount of) cocaine was removed from the formula in 1906. By this time medical concern about cocaine's harmful effects had reached the point where the Pure Food and Drug Laws (1906) banned the use of cocaine, and also opium, except for very small amounts to be used in prescription medicines.

Throughout history, societies and also individual users seem to have responded to cocaine in a similar way. At first the drug is thought to be wonderfully stimulating and free of unpleasant aftereffects. Beginning users feel sure they can control their cocaine use. But as the use of the drug progresses, serious mental and physical problems follow. Thus the medical profession's early hopes for the healing powers of cocaine gradually changed to severe concern about its threat to health.

As a result of the surge in illegal drug use of all kinds in the 1960s, millions of Americans have been exposed to cocaine. Because of cocaine's high price, its use tended at first to be limited to adults who could afford it. Because cocaine was taken up by certain athletic and show-business celebrities, and by well-to-do business figures and professionals, cocaine for a time was glamorized as a "rich man's drug."

Despite its expense, however, cocaine quickly found its way to the school-age population. By 1975 one in eleven high school seniors surveyed indicated they had tried cocaine at least once in their life. Ten years later, in 1985, that figure would nearly double. In the same ten-year period, the number of high school seniors who reported using cocaine over the past year more than doubled, and the number who reported using the drug in the prior month more than tripled. The same government survey reporting these figures also indicated that by age twenty-seven, nearly 40 percent of the population has tried cocaine. But the year 1985 was the peak year for cocaine use among high school students, and it began to decline in subsequent years.

Cocaine may be taken a number of ways: by placing it against smooth tissue in the mouth or elsewhere, by sniffing it in powder form, by injecting it into veins, or by smoking it. Until recently the most common method of cocaine use among Americans was to form small "lines" of the powder on a smooth surface and then to inhale them into the nostrils. In the 1980s, smoking a chemically purified form of cocaine ("free base," "rock," "crack") became increasingly popular among young users.

Users report that they experience a cocaine high much faster and more intensely when they smoke it in *free-base* form, usually called crack. Crack cocaine smokers also have a harder time than "sniffers" do in controlling their use. Crack users say that the drive to repeat the high is often irresistible; they stop only when their supply runs out. Crack was the growth drug of the 1980s. It spread most rapidly in inner-city areas among young people. Some drug experts believe that in the early 1990s, the number of people trying crack for the first time is beginning to drop. Statistics are not yet available to prove this.

Despite its popularity, cocaine has proven a serious threat to health and to life. The peak pleasure experienced by cocaine users is relatively short—about twenty minutes—but it is so intense that users frequently ignore published or rumored health warnings. Cocaine causes a flood of pleasure-producing chemicals to be released in the brain. This release is felt by users as a sense of alertness, confidence, and well-being. After this feeling fades, the user begins to feel the loss of those pleasure-producing chemicals. Feelings of flatness, irritability, and hopelessness are common after cocaine use. As they continue to take the drug, users are likely to feel dizziness, blurred vision, irregular heart action, and extreme nervousness. Substantial weight loss and inability to sleep are common among regular users. "Sniffers" are likely to form ulcerous holes in the tissue between their nostrils. This tissue damage also results in chronic bleeding.

Cocaine was once thought to be deadly only in

very high doses, but recent studies have shown that even small, single doses may cause fatal heart disorders, vomiting, and convulsions. In general, a user's judgment is not very reliable when he or she is high on cocaine. The chances of a very toxic or fatal cocaine experience increase when the drug is smoked in free-base form.

The current rise of cocaine use produces billions of dollars in illegal revenue each year. Smuggling and dealing contribute to rising crime rates and to the corruption of police and other enforcement officials. Because coca paste and pure cocaine take up little space compared to, for example, marijuana, smugglers can make far more money per deal than they could carrying a bulkier drug. Despite the new high demand for this drug, the cocaine-producing countries in South America have not profited generally from the illegal industry. Because a coca crop will net a higher price than can be earned from grains or vegetables, food production in cocaine-producing countries has fallen off sharply. The smaller supplies of food available then sell for higher prices, so that the relatively poor populations of growing countries find themselves with less food available and higher prices.

The big money in cocaine is made by criminal suppliers, not by the farmers who harvest the crop. A kilo (2.2 pounds) of cocaine sold by a South American to a smuggler costs about $5,000. The kilo may then be sold to a dealer in Los Angeles or New York City for $50,000. By the time it is divided into ounces and grams for sales on the street, the original kilo may earn $100,000 or more.

While plentiful new supplies have brought the

This photo shows South American workers farming coca leaves. Often farming coca results in a decreased supply of food for the poor population of the countryside.

price down a little, cocaine is still relatively expensive. Cocaine is purchased on the street for about $2,500 to $3,000 an ounce. The drug is most frequently sold in grams, costing roughly $100 each. These figures may vary from place to place.

In whatever form it is taken, and in whatever quantity the drug is sold, the cocaine epidemic is far from under control. Once again, people who begin to experiment with cocaine are often convinced they can "handle" the experience, that they can "take it or leave it." When users do become dependent on the drug, they are unable to say when and how they lost control of their own use; cocaine somehow—often very quickly—becomes the center of their lives. Without question, cocaine has a dangerously reinforcing (self-rewarding) effect on the central nervous system. It is the only drug that laboratory animals willingly consume until they die. At present, telephone hotlines and medical facilities for people in trouble with cocaine are able to respond to only a fraction of those seeking help.

SOME ISSUES IN REVIEW

The overviews of alcohol, cannabis, and cocaine tell us a number of things about the effects of drug use on society. History suggests that almost every drug is used at first for specific reasons, such as an aid to religious rituals or as medicine. Later, when a drug's reputation for producing pleasure becomes known, its use is apt to become widespread. History also tells us that, at first, societies and individual users tend to regard drugs in a positive way—as a means to indescribable feelings of pleasure or, perhaps, as cure-all medicines. This early positive response to a drug tends to promote its widespread use, whether legally or illegally. As drug taking continues, however, users begin to experience the negative, toxic effects: personality changes, deterioration of health, dependency, and death. When a society starts to link these negative effects with the drugs that cause them, there is usually an effort to control drug use. Recognizing this historical pattern of drug use can help us decide what the most effective response to today's drug problem might be.

The British crown began taxing alcohol in 1643 and has maintained the right to do so ever since. And as noted earlier in this chapter, the early American government maintained the same right when it responded to the Whiskey Rebellion in 1794. The Marijuana Tax Act of 1937 aimed to abolish marijuana use altogether by banning the growing, selling, and pos-

This lithograph, dated 1846, reveals that the historical pattern of drug use, including alcohol, has been recognized for many decades.

session of cannabis. These kinds of taxes, combined with quality-control laws such as the Pure Food and Drug Act, serve to regulate social drug use.

Some people would like to see currently illegal drugs such as marijuana, cocaine, and even heroin made legal and then regulated by the government. The issues raised by the regulation approach to drug use will be discussed more fully in the following chapter.

Before the twentieth century, the approach to most kinds of drug use might be called nonregulatory. As we have seen, cannabis, cocaine, and other powerful drugs were easily obtainable by those seeking to make patent medicines or even soft drinks. It is only when society becomes alarmed about the toxic effect of drugs that it begins to regulate or to prohibit drug use.

Prohibition continues to be a controversial approach to drug-related problems. As we have seen, the prohibition of alcohol in the United States (1920–33) did not work effectively and was abandoned as a national policy. In its favor, it may be said that alcohol consumption and its related diseases declined while Prohibition was in effect. The Harrison Narcotics Act (1914), the United Nations Single Convention on Narcotic Drugs (1961), and various state laws that assign criminal penalties for producing, selling, or possessing drugs are examples of ongoing attempts to prohibit drug use.

SUMMARY: AN UNSOLVED PROBLEM

One reason drug use persists is that drugs make users feel good, and users often do not easily feel the problems created by drug use. Damage to cells and tissue—including permanent changes in the brain—are not experienced as pain, at least not at first. The teenager who has begun to smoke cigarettes does not feel the coating of brown tar already forming on his or her lungs. Reports of lung cancer, emphysema, and heart disease seem decades away—forever. The young drinker who feels an exhilarating buzz after a few quick beers may think he is more alert as he pulls his car into traffic; others may suffer from the drinking driver's loss of coordination, but the drinker himself is likely to feel fine. Marijuana and cocaine users feel certain that chemical dependency is something that happens to others; after all, they argue, they are still in school, still holding a job—they are doing fine. When users are confronted with problems stemming from their drug use, they are likely to get angry, to deny that their use is a problem. They may claim that drug use is their "personal choice," their "life-style." The drug problem continues because users don't recognize, they deny, the damage they are doing themselves.

Once again, the pleasurable "payoff" produced by drugs is probably the key to understanding their impact on society. Pleasure rewards behavior. Just as a sudden cheer rewards completing a touchdown pass, and a delicious taste rewards eating a favorite dessert, a chemically created rush of pleasure rewards drug taking. Human beings, like all other animals, tend to repeat behavior that produces pleasure and to avoid behavior that produces pain. The greater the feeling of pleasure, the stronger will be the desire to repeat it and the more willingly a person will ignore or deny the risk and danger of the activity.

Even when the user's behavior is obviously changing and he or she has become very sick, those losses are "rewarded" by the pleasurable feeling drugs deliver. But again, once a user passes into a dependent condition, drugs deliver no more pleasure; they are taken only to relieve unbearable pain, tension, and feelings of guilt or hopelessness. The fact that drugs reward the loss of human performance and health *is* the "drug problem." Those who have not tried pleasure-producing drugs and who have learned about their toxic effects cannot imagine why anybody would start to take them.

For the reasons discussed above, reversing widespread drug use is not easy. It is especially difficult in a society that values individuality and privacy and which maintains that an individual's pursuit of happiness is an "inalienable right." Is drug taking a legitimate expression of a person's pursuit of happiness? The ways modern societies have approached this question will be the subject of the following chapter.

REVIEW QUESTIONS

1. What were the general patterns of drug use in the ancient world?
2. How was alcohol regarded by religious and government authorities in earlier times?
3. How did the United States' initial toleration of alcohol turn into a movement toward national Prohibition?
4. Why was Prohibition (1920–33) largely ineffective? Did the policy have any positive effects?
5. Why is there a greater concern about children drinking alcohol than there is about adult use?
6. When was cannabis first used as a drug? What were the results?
7. Why has scientific research on cannabis appeared only recently? What are some of the most important findings?
8. How is cannabis stored in the human body? Why is its storage a special health concern?
9. What were the ancient uses of coca? How effective was the newly discovered cocaine as a medicine?
10. What is the pattern of response to cocaine use—both by individuals and by society as a whole?

11. Is there a common pattern to the ways alcohol, cannabis, and cocaine have affected society? Explain.
12. Why do drug users resist warnings about drugs' threat to health, safety, and public welfare?

2 | Contemporary Debate

Do people have a right to use drugs?
How does drug use hurt nonusers?
When are you old enough to drink?
What's wrong with a little drug use?
What if drugs were legal?
What have alcohol and tobacco use taught us?
Aren't some drugs good for you?
Drug testing—does it invade privacy?

WHOSE BUSINESS IS DRUG TAKING?

Now that we have taken a look at history, we can explore some contemporary issues relating to drugs and drug use. Looking at the different positions people hold on these issues can help in deciding how each of us will respond to today's drug problem. The goal of this chapter is not to tell you what the right answers to the questions are. Often, there is no single right or wrong answer. Rather than telling you, the evidence is presented; you can think about your own position on these issues.

As we have seen in the previous chapter, drug use causes problems. Some of the problems affect the user alone: he or she may lose a job, become ill, develop a chemical dependency. Other drug-related problems affect nonusers and society as a whole. A doctor's or a mechanic's drug use may affect the health and safety of patients or customers. People who use drugs, especially those who are chemically dependent, are more likely than others to cause highway accidents, to commit crimes, and to fail to provide for their dependents. In some respects, drug use may seem to be a person's own business. But in other ways, drug use is clearly everybody's business. An airline pilot's use of alcohol or other drugs is obviously more than just a personal matter; the airline itself, the flight crew, the passengers, and even people on the ground may be affected by the pilot's "personal" decision to become intoxicated.

IS DRUG USE A VICTIMLESS CRIME?

Some people who have thought seriously about drug abuse in society believe that it is a mistake to make laws and policies against drug use itself. It is better, they argue, to outlaw the harmful effects of drug use. According to this viewpoint, the police might eject a rowdy drunk from a public concert and a marijuana-smoking salesperson might be fired from her job for absenteeism or for poor sales performance. But drinking and marijuana use in themselves should not be punished. People who hold this opinion think that drug users who can function on the job and who otherwise live within the law should be entitled to pursue drug pleasures if they please. Drug use, according to this position, is a victimless crime.

Opponents to the victimless-crime position argue that there is always at least one victim of drug use: the user. In the short run, drugs make users less able to control their actions and therefore more likely to do something harmful—to themselves and to others. Few would argue, for instance, that airline pilots should be allowed to use drugs. In the long run, the user's health, decision-making ability, and behavior will be affected by drug use. The lives of users will be shortened, and a predictable percentage of them will become chemically dependent.

Moreover, the argument continues, drug users become models for children and others to imitate. Children who take up drugs because of the appealing example of other drug users may be considered victims of drug use.

The saddest victims of drug use are the children of women who used drugs while pregnant. The federal government estimates that about 325,000 newborn babies each year have been exposed to drugs prenatally (before birth). Mothers of about one-third of these babies were crack users. In New York City, about 22,000 newborns were exposed to crack between 1985 and 1989. Such children are more likely to suffer from cerebral palsy than other infants. When "crack babies" enter school, they show short attention spans and greater incidence of hyperactivity. Many will need special education classes. The extra expense for their education and medical care may require hundreds of millions of dollars by the year 2000.

The victimless-crime debate raises the question of where a drug user's personal responsibility stops. Is the individual solely responsible for his or her own health, or do family and friends and society also have a say? Many people endanger their health by eating a poor diet; others take up risky sports like skydiving

Children often take up drug use because they see older role models, including their parents, abuse drugs. This can cause drug abuse to pass from one generation to the next.

and race-car driving. Why shouldn't people be allowed to endanger their health voluntarily by taking drugs? In other words, doesn't political freedom include the freedom to harm oneself? Or at least to risk harming oneself?

Experts who value freedom but who also oppose drug use tend to answer these questions in the following manner: Real freedom does include the right to do risky things and even to make serious mistakes. But a person is always responsible for taking the consequences of risky or mistaken behavior. Drugs, however, pose a special threat to freedom. For, while a person's initial decision to experiment with drugs may be a "free choice," that freedom is lost—perhaps forever—as drugs take their chemical effect. The real question is then "Should a person be free to choose a drug that is known to destroy the very capacity to make free choices?"

WHAT IS THE BEST LEGAL AGE FOR USING ALCOHOL OR OTHER DRUGS?

Even those who believe a person's decision to use drugs is his or her own business usually agree that drug use should be restricted to people who have reached a certain minimum age. At present most states have imposed a legal drinking age of twenty-one, while a few states allow drinking at eighteen or nineteen. In some western European nations, beer and wine can be purchased at sixteen. Which age is best? Which results in the least personal and public harm?

Those who support the higher drinking age point out that states that have recently raised the age limit to twenty-one are recording fewer drunk-driving arrests, accidents, and fatalities among young drivers. In the United States, the eighteen-year-old minimum age is often criticized because most high school students turn eighteen in the course of their senior year. If they are legally able to buy and to drink alcoholic beverages, the likelihood of their providing them to younger friends is fairly high.

Those who argue for a younger drinking age point out that in almost every other respect eighteen-year-olds are legally adult. They may legally vote, and if they break the law, they are tried and sentenced as adults. Eighteen-year-olds may also fight in the army, and many of them have full-time jobs. Shouldn't voting, wage-earning citizens be allowed to purchase a beer at a ballgame or a bottle of wine for a party?

To encourage states with lower legal ages to raise them, the federal government has withheld millions of dollars in highway funds from states that have not raised the drinking age to twenty-one. But because there are still a few states and some provinces of Canada that serve alcohol to older teenagers, carloads of young people travel across state and national borders in order to drink—resulting in a number of tragic accidents.

Whether it is eighteen, twenty-one, or some other age, most people agree that some minimum age should be reached before alcohol or any other drug is legally available. Growing children have not typically developed the personality controls that would enable them to drink safely. Physicians are concerned because the human nervous system is not completely developed until a person is past the teenage years. Thus children, including teenagers, tend to be influenced more by drug use than are more mature, stabler adults. Two ounces of alcohol (the amount in two shot glasses of whiskey, two cans of beer, two glasses of wine) can be a fatal dose to a five-year-old. The same amount can make a ten-year-old or a thirteen-year-old lose physical coordination and become nauseated. Alcohol (like other drugs) is generally harmful to health, and the more one takes and the younger the user is, the more harmful it is.

Those who have studied underage drinking closely and those who work with teenage alcoholics have found that underage drinkers reveal a special drinking pattern. Underage drinkers do not normally set out to have *a* social drink together. They are more likely to set out to get drunk—and will drink as much as it takes to do it. Underage drinking is also most likely to take place in secret, at times and places where adults will not be present.

Unsupervised, against-the-rules drinking is espe-

Avoiding heavy alcohol use as a young person is particularly important in order to avoid dangerous health effects.

cially likely to lead to other reckless behavior. Another concern about underage drinking—and about underage tobacco use—is that it accustoms children to breaking the law. Children who have already made the decision to drink or smoke illegally will feel less resistance later to such illegal drugs as marijuana and cocaine.

At present, there is disagreement about what is the best legal age for using alcohol. For obvious reasons, a single age at which young people could vote, marry, serve in the army, and drink alcohol is an appealing idea. But for the reasons discussed above, it is not always clear what that single age should be. Like driving, drinking safely requires a certain degree of maturity and judgment. Because individuals mature at different rates, some teenagers are ready to drive skillfully and responsibly at sixteen, while others are not. The same may be said about drinking. A few sixteen-year-olds, and perhaps many eighteen-year-olds, may be able to drink moderately and safely, but many are not. The fact that there are millions of adult alcoholics in the United States shows that a sizable percentage of drinkers of any age are not able to manage the use of alcohol.

Unlike driving, drinking changes the user chemically. Someone who drives recklessly and gets a ticket or who survives an accident may change his mind about the way in which he operates an automobile in

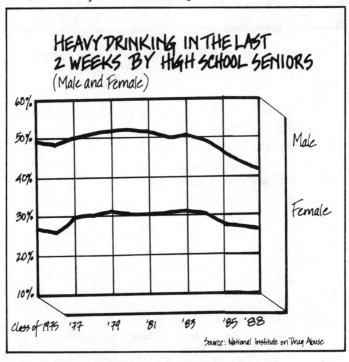

HEAVY DRINKING IN THE LAST 2 WEEKS BY HIGH SCHOOL SENIORS
(Male and Female)

Source: National Institute on Drug Abuse

The graph above contrasts the number of boys and girls who report heavy drinking (five or more drinks in a row) in the past two weeks. The results indicate that 1. high school boys are more likely to be involved in heavy drinking than are girls, 2. the number of boys and girls who drink heavily has stayed relatively the same over the past ten years, and 3. significant numbers of both boys and girls are involved in heavy drinking.

the future. Drinkers, however, have chemically altered their minds with alcohol. Any judgment a drinker makes is affected by alcohol. In this important respect, driving and drinking are not similar activities.

Whatever is finally decided about the legal drinking age, the most recent national surveys report that 85.3 percent of high school seniors have used alcohol in the past year. For those who try alcohol and other drugs, the age of "first use" is usually between the ages of twelve and sixteen. Few policymakers think that children this young should be allowed to use alcohol legally.

WHAT IS WRONG WITH "RECREATIONAL" DRUG USE?

Critics of federal, state, and local laws that ban the production and use of drugs claim that drug "use" is not necessarily a problem; drug abuse is the problem. They argue that, statistically, only a minority of people who use alcohol and such illegal drugs as marijuana and cocaine go on to become chemically dependent. They add that many of those who do become chemically dependent have a genetic (inborn) tendency to become dependent or that chemically dependent people have an underlying psychological problem that makes them rely on drugs in order to cope. Ordinary people, they conclude, can use drugs moderately, without necessarily harming themselves or others. Such people are said to be *recreational drug users*, as opposed to *drug abusers*. Those who approve of recreational drug use generally prefer laws, policies, and treatment programs that try to limit abuse, but not the use, of drugs.

Many drug-abuse specialists, national parents' organizations, and educators strongly oppose the idea of recreational drug use. Altering the brain with toxic chemicals, they state flatly, is not recreational; drug use is not comparable to engaging in sports, exercise, or hobbies. Moreover, they challenge the claims that there are "safe" use patterns of illegal drugs. Chemical dependency is a progressive (steadily increasing) disease. Many beginning users progress to occasional recreational use, then to regular use and dependency. Very few chemically dependent people believed they would become dependent when they started. These critics also link the permissive attitude about illegal drugs to declines in productivity in industry, to drops in American school performance, and to rising juvenile crime rates.

Foes of recreational drug use claim that the rise of treatment facilities for drug abusers has not reduced the total number of abusers. Simply treating the worst cases does not solve the problem. Statistical studies comparing drug use in different nations reveal that a consistent percentage of people who use drugs will become dependent on them. The only remedy proven to reduce drug abuse is to reduce the total amount of drug use.

Therefore, discouraging young people from trying illegal drugs in the first place and cracking down legally on those who do are the strategies preferred by those opposed to recreational use of drugs. Without use, there can be no abuse. Those supporting a no-use policy believe that the resulting gains in health, productivity, and learning will far outweigh the benefits of illegal, chemically induced pleasure.

IS DECRIMINALIZATION OR LEGALIZATION THE ANSWER?

The rise of illegal drug use that began in the 1960s was accompanied by the growing opinion that drug use should be legalized. This feeling was especially strong through the middle 1970s when the existing research on such drugs as marijuana and cocaine did not point clearly to health hazards. Those who favored legalization thought that certain drugs could be used responsibly by most people. By arresting and punishing such people, society made technical criminals out of people who would otherwise be law abiding. In other words, they believed most drug use was a victimless crime.

Books and editorials were written, calling existing drug laws a "new Prohibition." Pro-drug demonstrations such as marijuana "smoke-ins" were organized. Public disregard of antidrug laws continues today at rock concerts, sporting events, and other large gatherings.

Some of the arguments for legalizing the sale and possession of drugs have been made on economic grounds. Staggeringly large sums of money—perhaps a $100 billion annually—are generated by the illegal drug trade. All of that money escapes direct taxation. If an excise tax, like the one placed on alcohol and tobacco, were placed on drugs, billions of dollars would become available for public projects.

The government regulation of drugs would also require producers to set standards of potency and purity for the drugs they sold. At present, drugs sold on the street vary widely in their composition. Many people who think they are buying cocaine actually get some lookalike substance, such as amphetamine powder ("speed") instead. Cocaine is also cut (diluted) by adding other substances, some of them more toxic than cocaine. Marijuana sold on the streets is likely to include dirt, herbicides, and a variety of fungi. The amount of THC (the chief mind-altering ingredient) in marijuana also ranges widely, from almost nothing to amounts that can cause extreme body changes and hallucinations. All these problems could be avoided, according to those who favor legalization, if drugs were taken out of the hands of criminal suppliers and turned over to the government.

To move suddenly from outlawing drugs to a new system allowing their use would require a radical change in public opinion. Some people see decriminalization of drugs as a gradual first step toward making drug use legal. *Decriminalization* means removing criminal penalties for producing, selling, or using drugs. At first, the decriminalization movement aimed at removing penalties for marijuana use, since marijuana was thought by many to be less harmful than narcotic drugs such as heroin. A Washington, D.C.–based organization called National Organization for the Reform of Marijuana Laws (NORML) has worked nationwide to convince communities, state legislatures, and the federal government to change their marijuana laws or to get rid of them altogether.

For about a decade, in the 1960s and 1970s, decriminalization gained considerable support across the nation. In states that required prison sentences for possessing a marijuana cigarette, reform was probably overdue. Several states removed criminal penalties for possession of a ounce or less of marijuana. In

those states marijuana use was reduced from a felony
(a serious crime, carrying with it possible jail terms)
to a misdemeanor (a lesser offense). In 1975, Alaska
became the first state to lift all penalites for possessing small amounts of marijuana for personal use. In
California, where a considerable amount of marijuana is harvested illegally, a 1977 referendum called
for legalization of homegrown marijuana for personal
use. As recently as 1986, a state referendum in Ore-
gon asked voters to decide if the general harvesting
of marijuana should be made legal. The issue stirred
up passionate debate before Oregonians voted it
down.

In the 1980s the tide appeared to turn against
decriminalization and legalization of drugs. The rea-

_This photo, taken in 1972, shows a NORML conference in
Washington, D.C._

son for this may be that in 1979 and 1980, drug use by school-age children reached an all-time high in the United States. In schools, families, and treatment centers, drug-related problems were not going away. New and persuasive scientific findings on the harmful effects of marijuana and other drugs were beginning to convince doctors that drug use, especially by growing children, could no longer be taken lightly. The government's "war on drugs" also heightened the public's concern about the danger of drugs.

In 1974 Dr. Robert DuPont, a prominent psychiatrist and a former White House drug-abuse adviser, favored decriminalization of marijuana possession (although he was opposed to marijuana use generally). Ten years later, Dr. DuPont would write:

> I now reject decriminalization as a dangerous concept. After thirteen years of government service, the single biggest regret I carry is my naive support for decriminalization of marijuana. As I watched the marijuana-use figures double between 1974 and 1978, I felt the pain of regret with even greater force.

The most influential advocate of legalization as a solution to the country's drug problem was Kurt Schmoke, mayor of Baltimore. But he won few adherents to his view. A 1990 poll by the Bureau of Justice Statistics showed that 65 percent of Americans believe that the result of legalization would be an increase in the number of addicts and increased drug use in the schools. At present, the public appears to be opposed to legalization as an answer to the drug problem.

Critics believe that decriminalization and legalization of drug use will create more problems than they solve. For example, decriminalizing marijuana possession while keeping its sale against the law is likely to increase the demand for the illegal drug. Users, no longer worried about getting caught with marijuana, are likely to buy it and use it more freely. This will stimulate more criminal dealing. From the standpoint of the organized-crime bosses, this is an ideal stituation: Demand for their products is legal, but the illegal supply is neither regulated nor taxed.

The possibility of government regulation of drug production and sales in order to produce more uniform, purer drugs also raises problems. For example, as we have seen, the amount of THC in marijuana is what makes it more or less mind altering. If marijuana were licensed, taxed, and sold under government supervision, how much THC should it contain? A half percent or less of THC would produce only mild intoxication (but plenty of lung irritation). Two percent of THC is enough to make a typical user high. At higher percentages, users are likely to be powerfully affected; many experts would say dangerously so. Presumably, the government would set some limit on the potency of marijuana, as they set limits on the potency (proof) of alcohol. But if the government limits the amount of THC in marijuana, criminal suppliers would be quick to provide more potent varieties, or "better stuff." Thus the criminal supply of dangerous drugs would continue.

Of course, the strongest arguments against legalizing drug use are made by people who do not want the use of toxic substances to increase any more than it already has. Legally sold drugs are generally more available to underage children than illegal ones are. Today, alcohol and tobacco are by far the most widely used drugs in the United States. Nearly twice as many high school students have at least tried alcohol as have tried marijuana. Legalizing marijuana and other drugs would, without question, increase the amount of underage use. And no influential pro-drug organization, including NORML, recommends making marijuana legally available to minors.

THE LESSONS OF ALCOHOL AND TOBACCO

As we have seen already, a number of drugs are legally sold and produced in the United States. Most of them have to be prescribed by a doctor, but some, like alcohol and tobacco, are available to anybody who has reached a certain minimum age.

Those who would like to see the legalization of all drugs point to alcohol and tobacco as proof that a society does not collapse when drug use is made legal. Each year, however, alcohol and tobacco use cause far more deaths than do all other drugs combined. So why are such harsh restrictions placed on other drugs? Legal regulation might produce positive benefits. Government policy, as we have discussed, requires alcohol and tobacco products to meet certain standards. Moreover, the legal sale of these drugs produces millions of tax dollars for state and federal projects. The legal regulation of drugs also provides an opportunity to warn users of their potential health hazards. An example of such warnings can be seen on any package of cigarettes or in any cigarette advertisement:

SURGEON GENERAL'S WARNING: Smoking causes lung cancer, heart disease, emphysema, and may complicate pregnancy.

Arguments that certain illegal drugs are no more harmful than alcohol or tobacco may also be used to oppose their legalization. In the United States, tobacco use alone is estimated to take 450,000 lives each year. Drunk drivers cause over 15,000 highway deaths each year. In addition, tens of thousands of others grow ill or die annually due to alcohol abuse. If these two legal drugs are the greatest killers, why put others on the market?

There is also a concern that such illegal drugs as marijuana, cocaine, LSD, and heroin alter brain and body function more intensely than alcohol and tobacco do. Illegal drugs are therefore more likely to lead to dependency—and to lead to it faster—than are alcohol and tobacco.

Few who look at the historical evidence would

Drunk drivers cause over 15,000 highway deaths each year.

conclude that alcohol and tobacco have a good or safe record. If anything, there is a growing movement in the United States to combat the harmful effects of alcohol and tobacco. Victims and surviving families of drunk-driving collisions have organized such national movements as Mothers Against Drunk Driving (MADD) and Students Against Drunk Driving (SADD). The aim of these organizations is to strengthen laws against drinking and driving. Airlines, restaurants, and many private employers are paying increased attention to the rights and comfort of nonsmokers. Breathing in tobacco smoke from other people's cigarettes, pipes, and cigars is called *passive inhalation*. Current research suggests that passive inhalation can threaten a person's health. This information has strengthened the position of those who feel it is a basic right to live and work in a smoke-free environment.

In summary, tobacco and alcohol use have had at best a mixed record. Because they are legally available to adults, they are the two drugs most frequently used by minors. Many fear that legalizing other drugs will increase an already unacceptable level of underage drug use. Finally, no other developed nation legally allows the manufacture or sale of drugs like marijuana, cocaine, LSD, or heroin to the general public. Therefore, the United States cannot look elsewhere to decide whether legalizing more drugs will increase or decrease the existing drug problem.

DRUGS AS MEDICINE

Because certain substances used as medicine are also abused as drugs, the public is sometimes confused.

It may clear up the confusion somewhat to recall our definitions of *medicine* and *drug*. A *medicine* is a substance taken to relieve the symptoms or pain of an illness or injury. A *drug* is a substance taken to produce pleasurable feelings.

As we saw in Chapter 2, nearly all of the "problem" drugs available today were first used as medicines. Some of the painkillers that come from the opium poppy, such as morphine, are still widely used in surgery and in other kinds of medical treatment. Because they act powerfully and pleasurably on the nervous system, such drugs can accidentally cause people to become dependent on them. A number of medicines prescribed to help people to sleep or relax (*sedatives*) also may lead to dependency. In fact, next to alcohol, prescription medicines may be the leading cause of chemical dependency among adults.

Sometimes a controversial street drug like marijuana attracts publicity because of its occasional use as a medicine. For example, in the early 1970s several researchers investigated marijuana's potential for easing the symptoms of an eye disease called *glaucoma*. Glaucoma causes the fluids inside the eye to exert harmful pressure on the optic nerve and other eye tissue. At its mose severe, glaucoma can cause blindness. In the short run, the THC in marijuana was found to open drainage vessels in the eye, relieving the pressure felt by glaucoma patients. Continued research, however, suggested that marijuana was not especially effective in treating the disease. For one thing, the relief in pressure lasted only for a few hours, and the condition did not generally improve. It was also observed that in addition to relieving pressure, the THC lowered the optic nerve's blood supply to undesirable levels.

Nevertheless, newspapers and magazines across the United States reported that marijuana had been found to be good for glaucoma. The courts even allowed one Washington, D.C., man to be issued weekly prescriptions of marijuana cigarettes for his glaucoma condition. Few physicians, however, recommended smoking marijuana, a compound of over 400 chemicals, in order to get the effects of one of them, THC. Taking THC capsules or placing THC drops directly into the eye would be more direct and safer procedures.

Even though it was not found to be a very effective eye medicine, marijuana has been used by some doctors to treat cancer patients undergoing chemotherapy. *Chemotherapy* is the use of powerful chemicals to fight cancerous growth. The chemotherapy treatment that fights cancer, however, often makes patients feel severely nauseated. Some critically ill cancer patients have found that marijuana relieves the nausea. Marijuana has this effect, scientists believe, because it blocks the brain's ability to "read" that there are poisons in the patient's system. The healthy response to those poisons would be to vomit them out of the system. But in the case of someone seriously ill with cancer, the benefit of relieving nausea is thought to outweigh the toxic side effects of marijuana.

The point of these examples is that for a healthy person, marijuana interferes with normal functioning. Even drugs that prove to be "good" medicine produce toxic side effects. This is why doctors strictly limit dosages and the length of time a patient is exposed to drugs. Drugs used as medicines may help people who are ill. Medicines used as drugs may injure people who are healthy.

DRUG TESTING

Few drug-related issues have raised more angry debate than the issue of drug testing. Until the late 1970s, there was no reliable, inexpensive way to prove that a person was under the influence of a drug other than alcohol. (Alcohol can be detected by a fairly simple test that analyses a person's breath.) Students in school, employees at work, and drivers of automobiles might be suspected of drug intoxication, but unless they were actually caught taking nonalcoholic drugs, it was difficult to know for certain.

By 1980, relatively simple, inexpensive urine tests were developed that could detect the presence of marijuana's THC and other drugs in the user's system. The new testing method was tried out experimentally in prisons, industries, and the armed forces. These early tests were not given to punish users, but to identify them, as a first step to requiring them to stop using marijuana.

These early drug-testing experiments encouraged the organizations that carried them out. The results appeared to be highly accurate. A California prison tested 10,000 convicts and parolees for marijuana use. About 40 percent, or 4,000, tested positive, that is, showed traces of marijuana in their urine. When they were interviewed, all but three of them admitted recent marijuana use. Industries that began testing for drugs discouraged drug use among employees. Drug testing quickly raised the hopes of large orga-

Tests that determine whether someone is drunk have been used for many decades. The test in this photo requires that the person close his eyes and touch his nose with his index finger. To test for marijuana use, a simple test is used that detects THC in the person's urine.

nizations who were aiming to combat such problems as low productivity, drug-related accidents, and absenteeism.

Since 1980, drug testing has been steadily increasing in private businesses, in sports, as well as in such public institutions as police forces, schools, and the military. The rise of testing, however, has been met by increasingly strong objections from those who believe the tests violate basic human rights.

Drug-testing programs can take a variety of forms. Some organizations send only known users, or those who are strongly suspected, for testing. If the results are positive (showing recent drug use), that person is helped, if necessary, to become drug free. Other approaches to drug testing can seem more threatening to those who may be tested. One popular—but controversial—approach is called *random screening*. It requires certain randomly selected people in an organization to submit samples of urine to be tested for drugs. The advantage of random screening is that only a limited number of tests have to be given at any one time. Businesses that have used random screening report that the simple fact that a person might be tested cuts down overall drug use significantly. Other organizations prefer to test everybody, then perhaps to follow up with random screening.

Critics of drug testing are concerned about how the test results will be used. Will they be used only to diagnose a possible problem, so that the person can be helped to correct it? Or will positive tests be used to punish or fire organization members? At present, the tests are being used both ways. Some businesses will not hire a person unless he or she is tested for drugs. Similarly, many urban police departments will not let training candidates join the force until they have been tested and found to be drug free. Many people are also concerned that the test results remain confidential.

Confidentiality is part of the controversy over drug testing: Should a senior in high school who works part-time and tests positively for marijuana use have an official school or employment record showing the test result?

Some critics hold that regardless of how the tests are used, they are not appropriate in schools or in the workplace. These critics argue that requiring all, or even some, members of an organization to submit to a test that may indicate criminal activity violates both their privacy and their legal rights. The Fourth Amendment to the Constitution guarantees citizens freedom from "unreasonable searches and seizures." Foes of drug testing believe that requiring a person to submit a sample of urine for drug analysis is an "unreasonable search." They also maintain that both general testing and random-screening programs violate the legal tradition of assuming a person's innocence until he or she has been proven guilty.

Drug-testing opponents also argue that a person's behavior and performance in the workplace should be evaluated, not his or her body fluids. The issue, they claim, is not whether a person has recently used cocaine or marijuana, but whether the person is driving badly or working unproductively. At present, the urine tests for marijuana use reveal only that there are some traces of the drug in the user's system, not how much. Such tests therefore show only that a person may have used a drug recently. The tests do not show how intoxicated the user is or whether he or she is unable to drive, perform on the job, and so on.

Finally, there is concern about "false positives." These are test results that, due to human error or to a flaw in the testing process, indicate drug use when there has been none. The cheapest tests do produce occasional false positives, but organizations who use such tests generally retest any positive sample at least once. When a person's hiring or firing is at stake, repeated positive tests are subjected to a more expensive, highly accurate form of testing called _gas chromatography_. Even those who favor drug testing recommend careful safeguards against false positives.

To summarize, people's beliefs about the value of drug testing depend on how serious people believe the current drug problem is. Having to urinate on demand for someone in authority can seem like an invasion of privacy. Outside of medical practice, nothing quite like it has been required by businesses and government before. But it is also true that not until the age of airplane hijacking and terrorism were all passengers subjected to a required electronic scan of their bodies and luggage. If a drug test is devised that is as quick and easy as the electronic scanners used on airline passengers, perhaps some of the resistance to drug testing will pass.

IN REVIEW

In spite of the growing conviction in the United States that drug use creates continuing problems that must be faced, there are not yet many widely agreed-upon solutions. Issues such as the best legal drinking age, the decriminalization or legalization of marijuana, and the desirability of drug testing continue to stir up debate. People disagree about the best drug laws and policies because they disagree on even more basic questions:

1. How bad is the problem—what does drug use really cost in health, productivity, and quality of life?
2. Is drug use without drug abuse possible?
3. Can we "contain" drug use at manageable levels, or will it spread?

The information necessary to answer these questions will most likely come from history—including recent history—and from scientific research. Societies' responses to drug use in the past may reveal useful clues to dealing with the current situation. Further scientific findings will also help clarify the debate on drug-related issues. There is usually a gap in time between the increased use of any drug and the widespread appearance of harmful results. For instance, studies of cigarette-smoking men and women revealed that lung cancer rates began to increase dramatically twenty-five to thirty years after smoking rates increased. Until the cancer rates became intolerably high, there was much more debate about whether tobacco was harmful or safe.

Some scientists believe that the full health impact of the rise in illegal drug use that began in the 1960s is only beginning to be felt. Accordingly, in the next few decades, the specific health consequences of using marijuana and other illegal drugs will be more easily seen.

For the present, the challenge to policymakers is to prevent drug-related problems before it is too late for individual users—and society as a whole—to recover. Strategies for meeting this challenge will be discussed in the next chapter.

REVIEW QUESTIONS

1. Should drug use be regarded as a personal decision, or is it a public concern? Can it be both? Explain.
2. What are the arguments for and against drug use as a "victimless" crime? Which are most convincing?
3. Considering the arguments on both sides, should the drinking age be eighteen, or older?
4. Will decriminalizing or legalizing drug production and drug use ease the drug problem in the United States? Explain.
5. What are the main objections to legalizing and decriminalizing drugs?
6. Does the legal availability of tobacco and alcohol prove that other drugs can be legalized without disastrous results? Explain.
7. Reviewing the evidence closely, decide whether marijuana is "good" for glaucoma. Is it "good" for cancer? Explain.
8. Does drug testing violate a person's right to privacy? Does it violate the Fourth Amendment?
9. In what circumstances would drug testing be most justifiable?

3 | Future Outlook

How do we solve the problem?
Can't we stop producing and importing drugs?
Can we educate a population to say "no" to drugs?
Where should society put its time and money in fighting drug abuse?
How high a national priority is fighting drug abuse?
What are the chances of winning the fight?

Whatever side a person may take in the debate over the best legal drinking age or the proper penalty for possessing marijuana, nearly everybody agrees that widespread drug use causes problems that must be faced. Health losses and chemical dependency are perhaps the most obvious problems, but other, harder-to-measure losses may have a greater impact on society in the long run. Drug-related declines in productivity and in the general quality of life threaten a nation's future well-being.

At present, the United States is still feeling the impact of a rapid rise of illegal drug use that began in the 1960s. Considering the millions of people involved and the billions of dollars exchanged annually in illegal drug transactions, the current drug problem is not likely to disappear quickly. However, as we discussed in the preceding chapter, there is growing public concern over the harmful consequences of drug use. This concern may well express itself in new and more effective drug policies.

APPROACHES TO THE DRUG PROBLEM

Reducing Supply

Perhaps the most basic way to confront the use of illegal drugs is to eliminate them at their source. Drugs that grow naturally can, once they are spotted, be destroyed directly. Cannabis plants, coca bushes, and opium poppies are periodically sprayed with herbicides. In addition to these direct measures, governments may use diplomacy to influence one another to crack down on the production and distribution of various drugs.

Drug supply is part of the problem.

Stronger efforts to intercept drugs being smuggled across national borders is another approach to reducing drug supply. However, catching smugglers is expensive. The United States has thousands of miles of coastal and land borders to monitor. Moreover, the volume of recreational and commercial travel is so great that the systematic checking of every car, truck, boat, plane, and passenger for drugs would be impossible. Over the past ten years, both individual states and the federal government have stepped up their efforts to stop drug smuggling, but they have not yet succeeded in substantially slowing down the illegal trade.

Part of the difficulty in trying to shut down drug supply is economic. The *Drug Enforcement Administration (DEA)* is the chief federal agency responsible for enforcing United States drug laws. The DEA is responsible for fighting drug trafficking within and across U.S. borders, for investigating illegal drug operations, and for overseeing the regulation of le-

This photo shows bales of marijuana being transported.

gally produced drugs. Its budget in 1986 was approximately $400 million. That may sound like a great
deal of money, but the street value of drugs smuggled into the country is estimated to be more than
$80 billion—or 200 times the amount the DEA has to
combat smugglers. The profits to be made in drug
smuggling—especially of cocaine and heroin—are so
high that smugglers who believe they are being pur-
sued by the Coast Guard or by other authorities are
often willing to throw their cargo overboard. Sometimes smugglers will even abandon a boat or a small
plane. A failed smuggling attempt is more than paid
for by the next successful one.

Throughout the 1980s, law enforcement was allot-
ted an increasing amount of money to wage the drug
war. President George Bush has continued the Reagan programs. In 1991, the United States spent $10.5
billion to combat the menace of drugs.

When there is more money to be made in a criminal
activity than there is available to stop it, bribery and
corruption are likely to follow. Government policymakers, customs officials, and police officers are periodically paid to look the other way from major drug
dealings. Another difficulty in combating drug supply was the development in the 1980s of *narco-
terrorism:* smuggling drugs to earn money to carry
out terrorist political activities. Such activities dem-
onstrate that drugs are still easily available to those
who decide to deal in them. Effective measures to
halt drug supply have not yet been devised by the
governments of today's drug-producing and drug-
consuming nations.

There has been some success in the past. Some
policies aimed at destroying drug supply have

worked. China's successful attempt to curb opium use and Japan's crackdown on amphetamines were accomplished, in part, by passing and enforcing tough laws against the illegal production and distribution of those drugs. These new laws include mandatory sentences for drug possession and long prison sentences for suppliers. While it is difficult to stop illegal drug traffic altogether, decreasing the supply may be a necessary part of the solution.

Reducing Demand

In the 1980s U.S. policymakers shifted their emphasis to the demand for illegal drugs. According to this approach, if the public can be educated to resist illegal drugs, there will no longer be a market for them—and supply will fall off as a result. Policies aiming to reduce drug demand include education programs for treating people with drug-related problems.

The Reagan administration's Anti-Drug Abuse Act of 1986 was an example of the federal government's new effort to reduce the demand for drugs. This act provided millions of dollars to help produce educational materials for use in schools. It also made money available for drug-related research, for treatment facilities, and for drug information to be made available to the general public.

Many educators believe that the most promising way to reduce the American people's demand for drugs is to begin drug education before people make their first, or threshold, decision to try a drug. Since national surveys show that most drug users begin their use in the middle school and early high school years, many people feel that drug education should

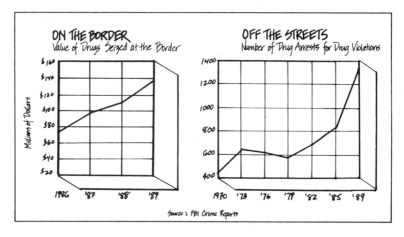

The statistics show recent results from national and local efforts to decrease drug supply (left) and drug demand (right).

start in the primary grades, in fact in kindergarten. These early drug education programs include lessons in which children learn to identify safe and dangerous substances. Children in primary school may also be given exercises in which they practice saying "no" to drugs and learn ways to get adult help in drug-related situations.

An attempt to stop drug use before it begins is called *prevention.* An effort to identify and to correct existing drug problems is called *remediation.* Remediation includes identifying and diagnosing people with drug problems, treating them (through counseling, hospitalization, or in specifically designed treatment programs), and helping them to stay "straight" (drug free) once they have stopped using drugs.

Both prevention and remediation are necessary in eliminating drug abuse, but drug-abuse specialists point out that prevention should be the primary goal.

Prevention is in the long run less expensive, more reliable, and much more pleasant than dealing with drug abuse once it has begun. Discouragingly high numbers of drug abusers who complete treatment programs fall back into drug use, and the rates are even higher for teenage abusers.

Nor is the outlook always bright for those who successfully recover from drug abuse. A number of doctors who specialize in drug-related illness have identified what they call a *Post-Dependence Impairment Syndrome (PDIS)*. PDIS is the tendency for former drug abusers to suffer from higher than normal rates of physical and mental illnesses. Alcoholics Anonymous (AA) has been the most active and effective organization in the United States in responding to chemical dependency. AA maintains that alcoholics and other dependents are never recovered, they are recovering. Recovery is a lifelong process that has to

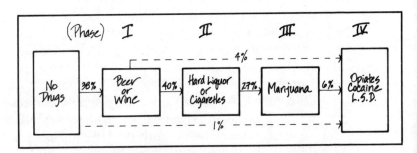

The diagram above, showing the results of studies published in Science *magazine in 1975 and in the* U.S. Journal of Drug and Alcohol Dependence *in 1980, indicates that high school users of alcohol are much more likely to go on to try other drugs than are nondrinkers. Similarly, this data suggest that those who try marijuana are far more likely to go on to other drugs than those who do not.*

be faced, according to an AA slogan, "one day at a time."

Another promising strategy for reducing the overall demand for drugs is to keep them out of the workplace. Just as creating drug-free schools has become a stated goal of many communities, creating drug-free offices and factories is a goal of an increasing number of businesses. Drug testing (pros and cons are discussed in the previous chapter) is perhaps the most controversial method of ensuring a drug-free workplace, but it is probably also the most effective. Many public and private organizations have also created *Employee Assistance Programs (EAPs)*, which provide ways for employees with alcohol or other drug problems to remain employed while they receive counseling, treatment, and support for staying drug free.

There are a number of other ways the private sector of the economy might, if it chooses to, help reduce the public's demand for drugs. Some of them were undertaken in the 1980s and early 1990s. Researchers have discovered that "secondary smoke," or the effect of smokers on others sharing a common space, is dangerous to the health of nonsmokers. As a result, many business offices have banned smoking or restricted it to restrooms. Some restaurants now require smokers to be seated in special areas. The airlines led the way in banning smoking on short flights, a policy that was then reinforced by a government regulation forbidding smoking on all domestic flights.

Other industries could do still more. Advertisers of legal drugs such as alcohol and tobacco could drop the youthful image of smokers and drinkers—for example, athletes relaxing with a cigarette after a workout. Producers of motion pictures and videos could make an effort to deglamorize drug use. Until very recently, the typical drunk in movies, plays, or television shows was portrayed as a harmless and funny character who suffered no serious consequences of his or her drinking. With the rise of illegal drug use in the sixties, a similar stereotype began to emerge—the superhip or funny burnout.

Because a number of drug-using celebrities were injured, became ill, or died over the past decade, there has been some change in the public image of drug users. Several popular entertainers and athletes have taken public stands against illegal drug use. There is little doubt that the entertainment industry's producers, writers, and performers have a sizable impact on the public image of—and therefore the demand for—drug use. Drug-abuse prevention experts regard it as a positive sign that Bill Cosby, a very popular prime-time television star, is willing to include clear antidrug messages in his show's scripts. Another move in this direction has been taken by MTV, the popular music video station. Its Rock Against Drugs campaign shows many popular rock stars urging their fans not to take drugs.

PERSONALITY PROFILE

Marsha Manatt Schuchard

If one person had to be named as having done the most to influence U.S. drug policy over the past ten years, Marsha Manatt Schuchard (Shoehard) might well be the person. As a result of her remarkable efforts, thousands of schools across the country have devised new drug policies, parents nationwide have organized themselves into informal community networks to prevent children's drug use, and community pressure has been put on merchants to stop selling drug paraphernalia and alcohol to minors. She has influenced state and federal lawmakers to stiffen anti-drug laws, and her work has been recognized formally by Ronald and Nancy Reagan.

Schuchard began with no special training—and no special interest—in the drug-abuse field. She is not a politician, a lawyer, a physician, a psychologist. Born and bred in Texas, she earned a Ph.D. in English literature and has studied and carried out research at several universities in the United States, Africa, and Europe. A resident of Atlanta, Georgia, she is also a homemaker and a mother. Her involvement in the drug-abuse prevention movement began when her eldest daughter became a teenager.

Schuchard noticed that a number of young people from her daughter's school acted dazed, distracted, and at times downright unpleasant during or after parties. After seeing used drug paraphernalia and bottles of alcohol at parties given by these young people, she realized that many students in junior high school and high school were getting drunk and stoned.

Disappointed, confused, and scared, Marsha Schuchard began phoning and calling on the parents of her daughter's guests. Most were shocked, doubtful, or angry that anyone would suggest their child was involved with drugs. Some parents felt that the party behavior, if true, was only normal adolescent experimentation. A few were genuinely concerned, however, and after much resistance, a meeting of the parents was held to figure out how seriously their children were involved with drugs.

The first meeting led to others—and finally to an agreement that parents should work together and with their children to prevent them from further drug use. The families reached a common agreement about weekday and weekend curfews, and they agreed to chaperone parties at their own homes and to check to see that the social gatherings their children attended were also chaperoned. The main point they agreed upon was that their children should be drug free.

This information organization, at first nicknamed the NPA (for Nosy Parents Association), took hold rapidly in Atlanta. Parents who were worried about their children's drug use, but who did not feel confident or well-enough informed to stop it, joined the parent groups enthusiastically. These same parents took their drug-related concerns to the Atlanta schools and succeeded in winning support for their drug-free goal.

Marsha Schuchard then launched a campaign to expose and close down drug paraphernalia stores ("head shops") in the city, and she took her findings and concerns to the Atlanta newspapers. She teamed up with Dr. Thomas Gleaton, a professor of physical education at Georgia State University and an equally energetic crusader against drug abuse, to form Parents Resource Institute for Drug Education (PRIDE). PRIDE quickly grew from a regional to a national organization that holds "how-to" drug prevention conferences for families, educators, and policymakers. PRIDE also acts as a national clearinghouse for drug information, books, and films.

Over the past decade, Drs. Schuchard and Gleaton have taken their case for a drug-free youth all over the United States, to Canada, and most recently to a number of underdeveloped countries.

Marsha Schuchard's book, *Parents, Peers, and Pot*, was published in 1979. Over a million copies have been distributed to date. Many public health officials feel that she has, without holding any formal office or position, changed the way the American people think about drugs. Her greatest gift may be giving parents confidence that they can be a positive influence on their children's drug-related decisions. She writes:

> It is difficult for adolescents to live in a loose, shifting family environment. In countless interviews with drug-troubled teenagers, one hears complaints about parents being hypocritical, inconsistent, permissive, selfish, or aloof, but almost never any complaints about strictness, rules, curfews, chaperones, or involvement. The number one and number two rules for today's parents should be "Don't be afraid to be a strong parent" and "Don't be afraid of your children."

A Systems Approach

Many close observers who have looked at the patterns of drug use in the United States believe that the drug problem will not be solved by confronting *only* demand, or by confronting *only* supply. People who use drugs are part of larger system; they are members of families, of schools, of businesses, of local communities, and of nations. Therefore drug policies should aim at every level of the system. Consistent programs to prevent and to treat drug abuse should be created for families, for schools, for the workplace, and for the larger community.

According to a systems approach, some policies would aim at reducing the demand for drugs through prevention and remediation; others would attack supply by political negotiation, tough laws, and improved law enforcement. As these combined efforts begin to succeed in reducing the supply and demand for drugs, the number of abusers—and the drug problem itself—will begin to shrink. If and when this occurs, time, money, and labor could be shifted from such activities as drug treatment and law enforcement to more long-term goals such as improved drug education.

SHOULD DRUG POLICIES AIM AT USERS OR ABUSERS?

What drug policies in the United States will look like in the future depends on how the "drug problem" is finally defined. Is the problem limited to the people who become ill, chemically dependent, or criminally involved with drugs? Or is the problem the fact that millions of people are using drugs in some form?

Those who believe that drugs can be used recreationally by the majority of users want to see drug policies limited to those policies that will prevent abuse. People who take this position also think drug education should teach responsible use of alcohol and other drugs, not forbid their use altogether. The minority of abusers should be treated by counselors and doctors the way any other sick person is treated.

Some spokespeople for this viewpoint also claim that if drug use were to become legalized, or at least decriminalized, the exciting "outlaw" aspect of drug use would disappear. If this happens, they argue, drug use will become less desperate and more a part of everyday life—it may even reduce the overall amount of drug taking.

Opponents argue strongly that any use of illegal drugs is abuse. They maintain, in addition, that children's taking of such drugs as alcohol and tobacco also constitutes abuse. They base their position on the fact that drugs have been proven to injure important human systems, including the brain, the lungs, the heart, and the reproductive organs. Drugs produce no positive benefits either to individual users or to society as a whole. Even the short-term pleasures for which people take drugs in the first place decline and disappear as use continues. A predictable percentage of every drug-using population becomes chemically dependent; therefore, the only way to reduce abuse is to reduce use. Moreover, there is no historical evidence that a developed society can successfully allow the recreational use of mind-altering drugs. Those who hold this no-use position point out that the legal drugs, alcohol and tobacco, are not only by far the leading killers, but also the drugs most frequently abused by children. Both the no-use and recreational-use camps tend to agree that children should not use drugs.

The no-use versus recreational-use debate must be resolved before consistent and clear policy can take effect. For example, no-use advocates want laws and policies that are tough on drug suppliers. They also favor educational programs with a clear no-use message to try to decrease demand. Recreational-use advocates think that police actions against most kinds of drug trafficking can be a waste of time and that responsible use should be the educational goal.

In the 1980s there was a shift in government policy and in public opinion toward getting tough on drugs. Future scientific findings about drug effects may strengthen antidrug feelings still further. But it is an open question whether drug use in the United States has progressed too far to be stopped.

THE FUTURE PICTURE

It is not an accident that the drug problem has become a central political issue for both major political parties in the United States. Although sensational events like the drug-related deaths of celebrities keep the drug issue in the public spotlight, the levels of illegal drug use remain alarmingly high.

While the link between drug use and other social problems is difficult to prove, the increase in drug use in the past twenty-five years has probably contributed to poor performance in the workplace and in school, and to the high rates of violent crime, infant mortality, and illegitimate births.

Is drug use the problem? Part of the problem? As they consider the question, both public and private policymakers have grown anxious to do something. What they do will depend, as we have seen, on how certain basic arguments are resolved. Those trying to judge the extent of the drug problem will have to review evidence. Some of the evidence is historical— how drugs have affected people in different or earlier settings. Some of the evidence is specialized and scientific. Other important evidence is less precise and harder to interpret—how drugs affect important everyday behavior, dress, speech, art, music, and values.

One of the greatest difficulties in interpreting the impact of drugs on American society over the past twenty-five years is that the phenomenon is still new; it is still happening. Historians will understand it better in a century or two. Nevertheless, some clear ·features of drug use since the 1960s can be identified, and these might be helpful to policymakers:

- *Drugs, once they are introduced, do not disappear by themselves.* The most popular new drugs of the 1960s, marijuana and LSD, did not replace or reduce the use of more traditional drugs such as alcohol and tobacco. Similarly, the recent rise of designer drugs (mind-altering synthetic drugs produced in laboratories) and cocaine has not replaced the use of marijuana or LSD. Use levels of the most common drugs have varied somewhat over the years, but no drug has dropped out of sight. In other words, drugs are added to, but not subtracted from, the illegal market.

- *When drug use levels off, it does so at a high ceiling.* In the early 1980s, some editorial writers expressed relief when national surveys showed that marijuana use by school-age children had declined. Other readers of the same figures saw little cause for optimism. For while the high school class of 1988 reported using marijuana less often (18 percent in the previous month) than did the class of 1980 (34 percent in the previous month), 33 percent of the class of 1988 still reported using marijuana at least once during the past year. The figure is still high enough to cause alarm among those who are worried about the long-term physical effects of marijuana. Moreover, while the percentage of high school students who used cocaine declined from 17 percent in the class of 1985 to 10 percent in the class of 1988, crack cocaine became a significant problem during the same period. No figures on crack use were collected before 1987; in that year, 5.6 percent of high school students reported using it. Despite widespread warnings about the drug, including an extensive ad campaign on television, the figure had declined only to 4.7 percent in 1989. The figures for alcohol have remained steady over the past decade, declining slightly from 93.2 percent of the class of 1980 to 90.7 percent of the class of 1989. Moreover, drug use among those of high school age may be even more prevalent than these figures show, for the surveys were taken among those actually in school. Thus, high school dropouts were not included, and most experts believe dropouts use drugs in higher numbers than those who stay in school long enough to graduate.

- *The drugs making the biggest impact at present are those that deliver quick and powerful pleasure.* The most rapidly advancing drug on the illegal market is cocaine. It generally delivers a period of peak stimulation lasting about twenty minues. Crack can be smoked to produce even more intense feelings— within seconds of inhaling the smoke. In addition to threatening the health and life of even occasional users, cocaine is currently proving to be a cause of epidemically large numbers of chemical dependencies.

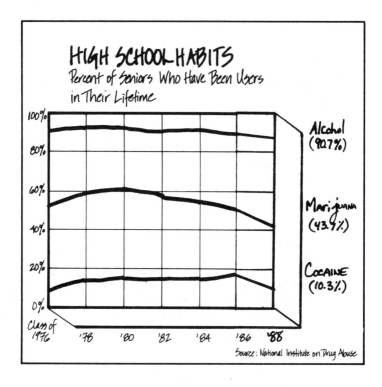

HIGH SCHOOL HABITS
Percent of Seniors Who Have Been Users in Their Lifetime

100%
80%
60%
40%
20%
0%

Class of 1976   '78   '80   '82   '84   '86   '88

Alcohol (90.7%)

Marijuana (43.7%)

Cocaine (10.3%)

Source: National Institute on Drug Abuse

- *Drug use has continued while other 1960s fads have passed on.* Illegal drug use may prove to be the most long-lasting result of the youth movement of the 1960s. Drug users in the sixties were likely to wear their hair long, to dress unconventionally, and to favor liberal or radical political causes such as refusing to fight in the Vietnam War, demonstrating for minority rights, and protesting the pollution of the environment. Today, young—and not-so-young— drug users are just as likely to dress conventionally, to be politically conservative, and to pursue careers in business and the professions. Times and styles have changed, but drug-use patterns still remain too high for the good of society.

BUILDING A SOCIAL CONSENSUS: A CONCLUDING VIEW

Open societies—those that allow opinions to be freely expressed—are occasionally slow to arrive at firm laws and policies. This has clearly been the case in the United States where drug policy has been concerned. Over the past two decades, drug users have tended to be defensive about their habits, often overstating the harmlessness of what they call "recreational" drug use. On the other hand, those opposed to drug use are often accused of interfering with the free choice and privacy of people who disagree with them. The majority of Americans probably stand somewhere between these two viewpoints.

Further scientific and medical findings may shift the balance of public opinion. Future drug scandals and tragedies may also have an effect. The most promising source of agreement right now is that *children* should be drug free. Policymakers, liberals and conservatives alike, have shown support of the idea of drug-free youth and drug-free schools. A broad social consensus about the benefits of raising drug-free children could very possibly grow into a large consensus about drug policies in general. There is the hope in many communities that teaching children to say "no" to drugs will change the future drug climate of the adult community.

Confronting and reversing drug traffic in the United States will not be pleasant, nor will it be easy. Confronting drug suppliers effectively will require expensive and possibly violent police actions. It will

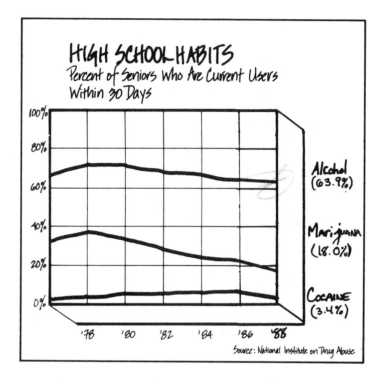

HIGH SCHOOL HABITS
Percent of Seniors Who Are Current Users
Within 30 Days

Alcohol
(63.9%)

Marijuana
(18.0%)

Cocaine
(3.4%)

Source: National Institute on Drug Abuse

require showdowns with organized crime figures. It may require drug testing and searching procedures, which most Americans are not used to. It will require school time and new classroom materials. All of these measures, whether carried out by public or private organizations, will cost money. Again, no effective action is likely without a strong consensus that the drug problem must be faced, that it will not go away by itself.

In one important respect, drug use is unlike other social problems. Drugs chemically change the thinking and personalities of the people who use them.

Even the ability to judge whether a drug is having a harmful effect is affected by the drug that is taken. If a large enough percentage of a society uses drugs, that society will have weakened its ability to evaluate the negative effects of drug use. If drug use progresses too far, it is possible that a society will find itself unable to reverse the process.

No modern industrialized country has fallen into widespread drug use and then made a successful adjustment to it. If the United States does so, it will be the first and may provide an example for other nations with similar problems. Whether the United States will tolerate or eliminate future drug use cannot yet be guessed. A number of informed observers, however, believe that the quality—if not the very existence—of life in the United States depends on which course is taken.

In the past, the United States has shown an impressive willingness to take on and to correct widespread social problems. A massive wave of political reform at the turn of this century resulted in cleaner, more sanitary urban housing and safer workplaces. The loss of national productivity and public morale caused by the Great Depression of the 1930s triggered many imaginative and effective changes in the nation's economic system. The drug problem, too, could very well provide an opportunity for a great step forward in public health.

REVIEW QUESTIONS

1. Why hasn't the U.S. government been more effective in eliminating the supply of illegal drugs?

2. What are the government's strategies for reducing the demand for drugs? Would time and money be better spent on prevention or remediation of drug problems?

3. What are some policies that private organizations could adopt voluntarily that might help reduce drug abuse?

4. How does a "systems" approach to drug abuse differ from the measures currently being taken?

5. What are the main obstacles to a consistent, effective national policy to prevent drug abuse? What is currently the most promising basis for agreement among all those interested in improved drug policies?

6. How has drug use in the United States affected the overall quality of life? Be specific.

7. What is the current "drug picture" in the United States?

8. What special advantages and disadvantages does an "open society" have in shaping future drug policies?

APPENDIX

RESOURCES

Al-Anon and Alateen

What about the family members and close friends of the alcoholic? It is easy to understand how alcoholism can destroy the alcoholic. Many ignore the fact that alcohol problems deeply affect the people close to the alcoholic as well. The purpose of Al-Anon and Alateen is to provide a support group where relatives and friends of alcoholics can share their experience, strength, and hope. Figures show that one out of every ten Americans develops the disease of alcoholism. Every alcoholic deeply affects at least four or five others. Many of these children, spouses, parents, friends and co-workers of alcoholics have formed the more than 30,000 Al-Anon and Alateen support groups throughout the world.

Al-Anon embraces all people who care about someone suffering from alcoholism. Alateen is for teens. If you are interested in learning more about either of these organizations, look up Alanon/Alateen in your local directory or write:

Al-Anon Family Group Headquarters, Inc.
P.O. Box 182
Madison Square Station
New York, NY 10159-0182

Alcoholics Anonymous (AA)

Alcoholism is a disease. It can hit people of any age. Alcoholics Anonymous is a worldwide organization of alcoholics who are dedicated to helping themselves and others stay away from alcohol. There are almost 67,000 local groups in 114 countries.

How does AA work? Members come together at regular meetings to share their experiences and support one another. All members come to the meetings of their own free will, because they want to stop drinking. There are no dues payments. Everyone is known only by a first name, so that everyone is anonymous.

In addition to the regular closed meetings, which are for alcoholics only, every group also holds open meetings for anyone interested. If you would like to get in touch with an AA group, look up Alcoholics Anonymous in your telephone directory. If there is no listing, write:

General Service Office
P.O. Box 459
Grand Central Station
New York, NY 10017

Mothers Against Drunk Driving (MADD)

One person can make a difference. After thirteen-year-old Cari Lightner died at the hands of a drunk driver, a Fair Oaks, California mother decided that something had to be done. She started Mothers Against Drunk Driving. Dedicated to supporting the families of victims killed by drunk drivers, and preventing further senseless deaths, MADD has had phenomenal success. In less than five years, MADD erupted from a one-woman organization to a nationwide, nonprofit corporation with over a half million supporters and members. Here are some of the accomplishments of MADD and the movement against drunk driving: Between 1980 and 1985, drunk-driving deaths dropped 20 percent. During that same time the number of drunk-driving arrests doubled. Most important, MADD's message is ringing all across America: *Don't Drink and Drive!*

How does MADD hope to end drunk driving in America? (1) It lobbies legislatures to pass laws to punish drunk drivers, prevent drunk driving, and help the victims of drunk-driving accidents. (2) It educates communities on the dangers of drunk driving. A number of its programs focus on youth. It sponsors programs to help junior and senior high school youth avoid dangerous situations involving the use of alcohol and other drugs. MADD sponsors poster and essay contests as well as student organizations. MADD also publishes "Student Library," a resource for drunk-driving information and creative ideas for student activities. If you are interested in getting involved with, or starting, a MADD program in your neighborhood or school, write Fran Hurtado, the MADD youth program coordinator at this address:

MADD
669 Airport Freeway
Suite 310
Hurst, TX 76053

Narcotics Anonymous

Most cities also have Narcotics Anonymous chapters. Similar to Alcoholics Anonymous, these support groups are made up of people who battle addiction to drugs. For more information, call or write:

Narcotics Anonymous
P.O. 9999
Van Nuys, CA 91409
(818) 780-3951

National Clearinghouse for Alcohol and Drug Information

Up-to-date information is vital for all Americans, young and old, who want to prevent abuse of alcohol and other drugs. If you want information about any type of drug problem, this is a great place to start. The NCADI provides information and services to anyone with questions or concerns about alcohol abuse, illicit drug use, misuse of prescription drugs, and other drug-related issues. Because NCADI focuses on problems of drugs AND alcohol, it is an especially useful resource.

If you have specific questions, call the clearinghouse library at (301) 468-2600. The librarians will be happy to find the information you need. If you are looking for pamphlets, booklets, posters, films, and videotapes, call or write the clearinghouse, which will send you the materials or tell you how you can get ahold of them. The NCADI will also be able to direct you to clearinghouses and information sources in your own state. Here is the address:

The National Clearinghouse for
Alcohol and Drug Information
P.O. Box 2345
Rockville, MD 20852

PRIDE (Parents Resource Institute for Drug Education)

What is "crack?" How is "crack" different from "coke"? How can you tell if your friend has a drug problem? If you want answers to these questions, but don't feel comfortable asking someone, call 1-800-241-9746 on weekends or at night, and an information computer will give you all the answers you need. (The phone call is free.) This phone resource service is offered by PRIDE, a worldwide organization headed by Dr. Thomas Gleaton at Georgia State University in Atlanta.

PRIDE also sponsors educational programs for parents and schools. Parents and kids must work together to stop street drugs, and PRIDE wants to help. The war against drugs is on; if you would like more information about

PRIDE's efforts, and especially if you are interested in bringing PRIDE's educational programs to your school, write:

PRIDE
100 Edgewood Ave.
Suite 1002
Atlanta, GA 30303

Safe Rides

As you can see, there are a lot of Americans, young and old, who are convinced about drinking and driving. Students at Darien High School in Darien, Connecticut decided to set up a free ride hotline. On Friday and Saturday nights, students volunteer to give free rides home for fellow students who have been drinking. Any student who has been drinking, or is afraid of traveling with a driver who has been drinking, can call the hotline and get a free, safe ride home. The program has made Darien, Connecticut a safer place and also given young people an opportunity to get involved and make a difference. With the help of the Boy Scouts of America, Safe Rides programs are spreading throughout the country. If you would like more information, write:

The Exploring Division
Fairfield County Council, B.S.A.
362 Main Avenue
Norwalk, CT 06851-1597

Students Against Drunk Driving (SADD)

Students can make a difference. In 1981, Mr. Anastas, the health education director at Wayland High School in Wayland, Massachusetts gathered together a group of students concerned about drunk driving. A sophomore student became chairman. They called the group Students Against Drunk Driving. In the past nine years SADD has spread through schools in all fifty states. The organization was founded for two reasons: First, injury from alcohol-caused crashes is the primary health problem among teenagers today. Second, SADD believes that these senseless deaths can be stopped. As the SADD slogan says, "If we can dream it . . . it can be done."

The program is designed to stop drunk drivers and save lives. Each of the more than 9,000 chapters tries to educate schoolmates and the neighborhood communities about the dangers of drinking, driving, and drugs. Chapters also organize peer counseling programs where students help other students who have concerns about drugs and alcohol.

SADD is made for students and run by students. If you are interested in helping start a SADD chapter at your school, talk to interested friends and teachers and write SADD for further information:

Students Against Driving Drunk
P.O. Box 800
Marlboro, MA 01752

Youth Groups

Do you want to get involved and learn more about drugs and alcohol? Do other issues, such as poverty, hunger, nuclear war, and pollution interest you? Perhaps you should join a youth group in your community. Synagogues, churches, the Boy Scouts, and the Girl Scouts are just a few of the organizations sponsoring active youth groups in your neighborhood. Through these groups you can participate in a number of these important issues. Youth groups are also a great place to find friends and meet supportive adult sponsors who want you to get involved. Give them a try!

TWO VOICES IN THE MARIJUANA DEBATE

In the following passages, two rival viewpoints are expressed about the safety of marijuana use. Dr. Robert DuPont is a practicing psychiatrist, a former director of the National Institute on Drug Abuse, and a frequent commentator on drug issues. Dr. Andrew Weil is a medically trained researcher on mind-altering drugs; his coauthor, Winifred Rosen, is a writer of children's books. Weil and Rosen's book, From Chocolate to Morphine, *is aimed at school-age readers. DuPont's book,* Getting Tough on Gateway Drugs, *is aimed at both children and their parents.*

From Chocolate to Morphine

When people learn to get high on marijuana, their early experiences with it are often quite lively. Everything may strike them funny, and all sensory experiences become novel and interesting. Listening to music, eating, and making love can become more than usually absorbing. Time seems long and drawn out. People sometimes have strange illusions, such as seeing a room expand or feeling as though their legs have become enormously long.

With repeated use, these remarkable effects tend to fade away. Regular users may find that pot makes them relaxed or more sociable without greatly affecting their perceptions or moods. Very heavy users usually feel little from the drug, often smoking it simply out of habit.

Bad reactions to marijuana are more likely when high doses of strong material are taken in bad settings, especially by inexperienced users. Most are simple panic reactions, easily treated with reassurance that everything will be all right as soon as the drug wears off. The effects of smoking marijuana usually diminish after an hour and disappear after two or three hours. Some people, if they have smoked a lot of pot, feel tired or "fuzzy" the next morning.

Some users find that marijuana stimulates them and

keeps them awake at night; others use it to help them fall asleep. It makes some people depressed and irritable, and others groggy for several hours. Possibly, some kinds of pot are more sedative than others. In recent years, stronger and stronger marijuana has become available. Some of the very potent sinsemilla ("without seed") from California is as potent as hashish and can be disorienting to people who are not used to it. . . .

The medical safety of marijuana is great. It does not kill people in overdose or produce other symptoms of obvious toxicity. Used occasionally, it is no more of a health problem than the occasional use of coffee or tea, and certainly it is less toxic than alcohol or tobacco.

Long-term, regular marijuana smoking can, however, significantly irritate the respiratory tract, causing chronic, dry coughs that resemble the coughs of some cigarette smokers. Further, marijuana smoke may contain more tars than tobacco smoke and can probably produce lung and bronchial disease in susceptible individuals. The risk depends on how much users smoke over how long a time.

Aside from respiratory irritation, heavy marijuana use does not seem to cause other medical problems. Of course, warnings of the medical dangers of cannabis have been well publicized, with reports of everything from brain damage to injury of the immune and reproductive systems, but these are based on poor research, often conducted by passionate foes of the drug. Studies of populations that have smoked cannabis for many years do not reveal obvious illnesses that can be linked to marijuana.

Getting Touch on Gateway Drugs

What Scientists Say About the Effects of Marijuana Use on the Central Nervous System. Against the background of possible cognitive failures and sensory distortions I have just described, I call your attention now to a number of relevant and significant conclusions reached by a panel of distinguished research scientists. Following through on a request from the National Institute on Drug Abuse and National Institute of Health, the Institute of Medicine of the prestigious, nongovernmental National Academy of Sciences prepared a comprehensive study on the health effects of marijuana use. The report, released in February 1982, represents a cautious, conservative review of the scientific evidence presently available. In a section on the "Effects of Marijuana Use on the Central Nervous System," the panel commented—in essence—as follows:

- Acute effects of marijuana smoking include feelings of euphoria, but use can also cause disturbing mental experiences, including short periods of anxiety, confusion, or psychosis.
- Marijuana impairs or interferes with short-term memory, slows the learning process, interferes with oral communication, and may trigger temporary confusion and delirium. These effects are of special concern because high-school students who use marijuana tend to use it during schooltime. The learning defect in particular persists for hours after the euphoria or high has worn off.
- Chronic, heavy use of marijuana is associated with behavioral and mental disorders in people.
- Marijuana has worrisome and sometimes harmful short-term effects on reflexes, physical effectiveness, and vision.
- Marijuana use significantly impairs motor coordination and the perceptual ability to follow a moving object and to detect a flash of light—factors which pose a substantial risk when driving a motor vehicle and operating other machines, including industrial machinery. These impairments and perceptual deficits can last four to eight hours after the actual high.
- The panel of experts, as a group, found it difficult to determine whether marijuana use is a cause or an effect

of the so-called "amotivational syndrome," which produces apathy, poor schoolwork, and poor job performance. The rise in marijuana use during the last two decades, however, closely correlates with the fall in Scholastic Aptitude Test (SAT) scores.

- So far, the panel concluded, there is no convincing evidence of long-term behavioral effects persisting after marijuana use stops, although it is also not clear that such effects do not occur. In other words, the jury is still out on this one.
- Marijuana and its byproducts can remain in the brain and other organs of the body for long periods of time, even months, with unknown but possibly subtle effects.
- Long-term effects of marijuana on the human brain and on behavior are not yet known, but the short-term effects are of sufficient import as to encourage and accelerate intensive research concerning possible long-term consequences.

Clearly, the negative effects of marijuana on the brain and the rest of the central nervous system, particularly as they affect learning, studying, and neuromuscular coordination skills like driving, ought to be matters of grave concern. This is especially urgent in a society like ours: a society that is knowledge-centered and that "runs on wheels."

On the day the National Academy of Sciences released its comprehensive report on the effects of marijuana use, I interviewed the chairman of the panel that prepared it. In the interview, which took place on a local call-in radio program, I asked him how he would have felt if he had known that the pilot flying the plane which took him back to Boston that day had been smoking marijuana before the flight, or even several days before the flight. He said he would not have wanted to fly on a plane piloted by anyone who smoked marijuana no matter if the smoking had occurred many days before.

NATIONAL INSTITUTE ON DRUG ABUSE REPORT, 1987

This report on drug use by young Americans, citing numbers shown in figures in the text, was issued on February 20, 1987, by the University of Michigan and the National Institute on Drug Abuse.

ANN ARBOR—The gradual decline in drug use by young Americans resumed in 1986—after a year's interruption—but well over half of all high-school seniors still report having had some experience with illicit drugs, according to researchers at The University of Michigan's Institute for Social Research (ISR).

A notable exception to the pattern of decline, however, occurred in the case of cocaine, which remained at peak levels among students despite increased public attention to its dangers.

Overall use of illicit drugs by American young people continues to be extremely high in comparison to other industrialized countries or our own past, the U-M investigators noted.

Reporting on the 12th national survey of nearly 130 high schools, ISR social scientists Lloyd D. Johnston, Jerald G. Bachman, and Patrick M. O'Malley said that the proportion of seniors indicating any experience with illicit drugs in their lifetime fell modestly, from 61 percent in 1985 to 58 percent in 1986. Prior-month use (that is, current use) was reported by 27 percent of the students in 1986, down from 30 percent in 1985.

"What is most significant about these results," Johnston said, "is that the stall we observed in 1985, in an otherwise continuous decline over several years, was just that—a stall. It was not the end of the decline, nor the beginning of a turnaround in drug use, as some had feared."

The proportion of seniors who have at some time used an illicit drug has now fallen from a peak of around 66 percent in 1981 to last year's 58 percent, a decline in lifetime use that Johnston describes as "rather modest." The decline in current use has been more sizable, a drop of nearly one-third from 39 percent in 1979 to 27 percent in 1986.

Significant declines were oberved in 1986 in the use of marijuana, amphetamine stimulants, and methaqualone. Usage rates were relatively unchanged for PCP, LSD, and heroin, drug classes whose use declined earlier and remains quite low. Long-term gradual declines continued in the use of barbituates and tranquilizers.

The proportion of seniors reporting prior-month use of marijuana fell from 26 percent in 1985 to 23 percent last year, a figure more than one-third below the 1978 peak level of 37 percent. Daily marijuana use was down from 5 percent in 1985 to 4 percent in 1986, but far below its peak of 11 percent in 1978.

Current use of amphetamines, once second in prevalence, stood at 5.5 percent in 1986, down more than half from a peak level of about 13 percent in 1981. Cocaine is now the second-most-used illicit drug among high-school seniors.

The 1986 survey showed no appreciable change from the prior year in overall use of cocaine. One senior in six (17 percent) had tried cocaine, 13 percent had used it in the prior year, 6 percent in the prior month.

"This is an instance where a lack of change is quite significant," Johnston explained, "because it means that cocaine use remained at peak levels in this group despite accumulating evidence of, and public attention to, its addictive potential and possible toxic effects."

While a majority of student respondents recognized great risk in occasional use of cocaine (54 percent) and regular use (82 percent), only about one-third (34 percent) saw experimenting with cocaine as endangering the user.

"As recently as last spring, a great many young people still seemed to think that they could play around with cocaine and not run much of a risk, even though an increasing number were coming to recognize that regular use is very dangerous," Johnston said. "Of course some dramatic events have occurred since the last survey was completed—including the untimely deaths of sports figures Len Bias and Don Rogers—which one would hope have had some impact."

While the proportion of high-school students using cocaine has not changed much since 1980, the investigators report some important qualitative changes.

Since 1983, they say, there has been an increase in the number of frequent cocaine users, an increase in the number of students who reported difficulty in discontinuing their use, and an increase in the number of students smoking cocaine, including "crack"—a potent, smokable form of the drug.

Daily use of cocaine roughly doubled between 1983 and 1986, from 0.2 percent to 0.4 percent, the highest level observed so far. Regarding increased dependence, the proportion of all seniors who said they used cocaine in the last year *and* were unable to stop using it at some time also doubled from 0.4 percent in 1983 to 0.8 percent in 1986 (0.8 percent corresponds to roughly 25,000 seniors nationwide).

"Certainly one reason for the increased rate of subjectively reported dependence is the increase in the proportion of students smoking cocaine," Johnston explained. "While the proportion of students indicating they smoked cocaine in the past year hovered around 2.5 percent between 1979 and 1983, since then it has risen steadily to reach 6 percent of all seniors by 1986.

"Undoubtedly crack has been an important contributor to the growth of this more dangerous mode of ingestion. While we will have more information on crack use next year than is available at present, what we do have indicates that this particularly dangerous form of cocaine has reached communities throughout the country. It is not confined to a few large cities, as many had hoped."

One senior in twenty-five or 4.1 percent confirmed the use of crack at least once in the year prior to the 1986 survey. One-third of all prior-year cocaine users had some experience with crack.

Crack users have a demographic profile similar to that of users of the powdered form of cocaine: Males are somewhat more likely to be users than females; use is higher in the Northeastern and Western regions than in the North Central and Southern regions, and use is higher in more urban areas than in less urban ones. The crack-user profile differs from powder cocaine in being even more concentrated among non-college-bound students.

About half of the high schools in the study showed some reported crack use. The highest percentage reported for prior-year crack users in a single school was 18 percent. Nonurban communities in the South appeared to be least affected by crack cocaine.

Johnston's assessment is that "crack has become available rather widely across the country, but the rapid and dramatic spread of public information about its dangers has helped to stem what might have been a much larger epidemic. Nevertheless, there is enough use out there already—and a sufficiently widespread availability—to be cause for continued concern."

In its look at the two major licit drugs, the ISR survey found little change in alcohol use in 1986 and only a slight drop in cigarette smoking.

Alcohol is widely and frequently used by high-school students. Nearly two-thirds of the seniors reported using it in the thirty days prior to the survey, 37 percent admitted having five or more drinks in a row at least once in the prior two weeks, and 5 percent reported daily or near-daily use in the prior month.

Johnston said, "Cigarette smoking among American teenagers dropped by about one-quarter to one-third some years back. But in recent years, there has been little further progress."

He noted that daily use of cigarettes fell from 21 percent to 19 percent between 1980 and 1985. The number of half-a-pack or more smokers was down slightly, which may be attributed in part to the proliferation of no-smoking policies in schools and workplaces.

"Nevertheless," Johnston said, "we seem to be making very little progress in reducing the onset of this deadly addiction among our children—an addiction which probably will cut short the lives of more of them than will all the others drugs combined.

"The fact that smoking rates among teenagers are changing so little is of particular importance, since it is during the teens that the vast majority of smokers establish their smoking habit. In fact, it is somewhat surprising that smoking levels are not dropping more among teenagers, considering the large changes in societal norms which have been taking place."

In commenting on the significance of the overall 1986 results, the investigators point out that while progress in reducing the use of illicit drugs was modest, it is encouraging. "The fact that illicit drug use overall is once again decreasing in popularity, albeit slowly, is the most encouraging part of the story," concludes Johnston. "But the fact that there is an increasing use of cocaine in its most addicting form is certainly a sobering counterweight. Further, the overall levels of illicit drug use by our young people remain extremely high, both by historical standards in this country and by comparison to virtually all of the industrialized world. In addition, we know that these adolescents will carry their drug habits into their twenties, as they enter the work force. Clearly, a great deal remains to be done."

SELECTED PSYCHOACTIVE DRUGS AND SCHEDULES ESTABLISHED BY THE CONTROLLED SUBSTANCES ACT, 1970

This schedule was issued by the Drug Enforcement Administration.

Schedule I

Substances with a high potential for abuse, and no currently accepted medical use in the United States. (Available for research purposes only)

Heroin
Psychedelics—LSD, Mescaline, Peyote, Psilocybin
Marijuana—in spite of recent studies indicating a variety of potential therapeutic uses, and THC, marijuana's active ingredient
Hashish

Schedule II

Substances with high potential for abuse, but such drugs have a currently accepted medical use in the United States, often with severe restriction. Abuse may lead to severe psychological or physical dependence. (Available by written prescription only; no refills)

Opium
Morphine
Codeine

Demerol
Methadone
Barbiturates
Amphetamines
Cocaine
Phencyclidine (an animal tranquilizer)

Schedule III

Substances with a potential for abuse less than drugs in Schedules I and II. Such drugs have a currently accepted medical use in the United States. Abuse may lead to moderate or low physical or high psychological dependence. (Available by written or oral prescription; 5 refills in 6 months with medical authorization)

Empirin Compound with codeine
Paregoric
Ritalin
Preludin
Glutethimide (Doriden)

Schedule IV

Substances with a low potential for abuse relative to drugs in Schedule III. These drugs have a currently accepted medical use in the United States. Abuse may lead to limited physical or psychological dependence relative to drugs in Schedule III. (Availability without prescription depends upon individual state laws)

Robitussin A-C cough syrup
Cheracol with codeine
Terpin hydrate with codeine

DANGER SIGNALS OF DRUG ABUSE

This document was issued by the National Institute on Drug Abuse.

Many people are prescribed drugs that affect their moods. Using these drugs wisely can be important for physical and emotional health. But sometimes it is difficult to decide when using drugs to handle stress becomes inappropriate. It is important that your use of drugs does not result in catastrophe. Here are some "danger signals" that can help you evaluate your own way of using drugs.

1. Do those close to you often ask about your drug use? Have they noticed any changes in your moods or behavior?
2. Are you defensive if a friend or relative mentions your drug or alcohol use?
3. Are you sometimes embarrassed or frightened by your behavior under the influence of drugs or alcohol?
4. Have you ever gone to see a new doctor because your regular physician would not prescribe the drug you wanted?
5. When you are under pressure or feel anxious, do you automatically take a tranquilizer or drink or both?
6. Do you take drugs more often or for purposes other than those recommended by your doctor?
7. Do you mix drugs and alcohol?
8. Do you drink or take drugs regularly to help you sleep?
9. Do you have to take a pill to get going in the morning?
10. Do you think you have a drug problem?

If you have answered *yes* to a number of these questions, you may be abusing drugs or alcohol. There are places to go for help at the local level. One such place might be a drug-abuse program in your community, listed in the Yellow Pages under Drug Abuse. Other resources include community crisis centers, telephone hotlines, and the Mental Health Association.

WHAT IS SOCIAL DRINKING?

This document was issued by the National Institute on Alcohol Abuse and Alcoholism.

Social Drinking Is

A glass of wine to enhance a meal
A drink or two while you are having fun
Sipping and eating

Using alcohol as a beverage
Drinking and talking with friends
Never having to say you are sorry for what you did while
    drinking
Knowing when to say when

Social Drinking Is Not

Three fast martinis before lunch
Having to drink to have fun
Gulping drinks on an empty stomach
Forgetting what you did while drinking
Drinking and worrying alone
Showing off how much you can hold
Using alcohol as a problem solver

Where does social drinking end and problem drinking
begin? There is no simple answer. However, here is one
good description: IF YOU NEED A DRINK TO BE SOCIAL,
THAT'S NOT SOCIAL DRINKING!

THE EIGHTEENTH AMENDMENT

*This amendment was proposed on December 18, 1917; declared ratified on
January 29, 1919.*

After one year from the ratification of this article, the manufacture,
sale, or transportation of intoxicating liquors within, the importation thereof into, or the exportation thereof from the United States
and all territory subject to the jurisdiction thereof for beverage
purposes is hereby prohibited.

The Congress and the several States shall have concurrent power
to enforce this article by appropriating legislation.

This article shall be inoperative unless it shall have been ratified
as an amendment to the Constitution by the legislatures of the
several States, as provided in the Constitution, within seven years
from the date of the submission hereof to the States by the
Congress.

THE SINGLE CONVENTION ON NARCOTIC DRUGS (1961)

The Single Convention on Narcotic Drugs is an international law passed by the United Nations in 1961. This lengthy document, parts of which are included below, was the result of the testimony of nearly 500 expert witnesses, most of them scientific and medical specialists. Seventy-four nations, including the United States, signed this agreement. It is the most recent and most far-reaching agreement on international drug traffic.

Review of this document will reveal several important drug-abuse issues, including: (1) which drugs are thought to be the greatest threat internationally, (2) how governments can be aware of the amount of drug traffic that is carried on, and (3) how governments hope to cooperate in enforcing drug policies worldwide.

A question to consider: If the following document were lost, and found in 1,000 years, what would it tell a reader about life in the twentieth century?

Preamble

The Parties,

Concerned with the health and welfare of mankind,

Recognizing that the medical use of narcotic drugs continues to be indispensable for the relief of pain and suffering and that adequate provision must be made to ensure the availability of narcotic drugs for such purposes,

Recognizing that addiction to narcotic drugs constitutes a serious evil for the individual and is fraught with social and economic danger to mankind,

Conscious of their duty to prevent and combat this evil,

Considering that effective measures against abuse of narcotic drugs require coordinated and universal action,

Understanding that such universal action calls for international cooperation guided by the same principles and aimed at common objectives,

Acknowledging the competence of the United Nations in the field of narcotics control and desirous that the international organs concerned should be within the framework of that Organization,

Desiring to conclude a generally acceptable international convention replacing existing treaties on narcotic drugs, limiting such drugs to medical and scientific use, and providing for continuous international cooperation and control for the achievement of such aims and objectives,

Hereby agree as follows.

Article 1. Definitions

1. Except where otherwise expressly indicated or where the context otherwise requires, the following definitions shall apply throughout the Convention:

a. "Board" means the International Narcotics Control Board.

b. "Cannabis" means the flowering or fruiting tops of the cannabis plant (excluding the seeds and leaves when not accompanied by the tops) from which the resin has not been extracted, by whatever name they may be designated.

c. "Cannabis plant" means any part of genus cannabis.

d. "Cannabis resin" means the separated resin, whether crude or purified, obtained from the cannabis plant.

e. "Coca bush" means the plant of any species of the genus eryhroxylon.

f. "Coca leaf" means the leaf of the coca bush except a leaf from which all ecgonine, cocaine, and any other ecgonine alkaloids have been removed.

g. "Commission" means the Commission on Narcotic Drugs of the Council.

h. "Council" means the Economic and Social Council of the United Nations.

i. "Cultivation" means the cultivation of the opium poppy, coca bush, or cannabis plant.

j. "Drug" means any of the substances in Schedules I and II, whether natural or synthetic.

k. "General Assembly" means the General Assembly of the United Nations.

l. "Illicit traffic" means cultivation or trafficking in drugs contrary to the provision of this convention.

m. "Import" and "export" mean in their respective connotations the physical transfer of drugs from one State to another State, or from one territory to another territory of the same State.

n. "Manufacture" means all processes, other than production, by which drugs may be obtained and includes refining as well as the transformation of drugs into other drugs.

o. "Medicinal opium" means opium which has undergone the processes necessary to adapt it for medicinal use.

p. "Opium" means the coagulated juice of the opium poppy.

q. "Opium poppy" means the plant of the species Papaver somniferum L.

r. "Poppy straw" means all parts (except the seeds) of the opium poppy, after mowing.

s. "Preparation" means a mixture, solid or liquid, containing a drug.

t. "Production" means the separation of opium, coca leaves, cannabis, and cannabis resin from the plants from which they are obtained.

u. "Schedule I," "Schedule II," "Schedule III," and "Schedule IV" mean the correspondingly numbered list of drugs or preparations annexed to this Convention, as amended from time to time in accordance with article 3.

v. "Secretary-General" means the Secretary-General of the United Nations.

w. "Special stocks" means the amounts of drugs held in a country or territory by the Government of such country or territory for special Government purposes and to meet exceptional circumstances; and the expression "special purposes" shall be construed accordingly.

x. "Stocks" means the amounts of drugs held in a country or territory and intended for:

    i. Consumption in the country or territory for medical and scientific purposes, or

    ii. Utilization in the country or territory for the manufacture of drugs and other substances, or

    iii. Export; but does not include the amounts of drugs held in the country or territory,

    iv. Use by retail pharmacists or other authorized retail distributors and by institutions or qualified persons in the duly authorized exercise of therapeutic or scientific functions, or

    v. As "special stocks."

y. "Territory" means any part of a State which is treated as a separate entity for the application of the system of import certificates and export authorizations provided for in article 31. This definition shall not apply to the term "territory" as used in articles 42 and 46.

2. For the purposes of this Convention a drug shall be regarded as "consumed" when it has been supplied to any person or enterprise for retail distribution, medical use, or scientific research; and "consumption" shall be construed accordingly. . . .

Article 14. Measures by the Board to Ensure the Execution of Provisions of the Convention

1. a. If, on the basis of its examination of information submitted by Governments to the Board under the provisions of this Convention, or of information communicated by United Nations organs and bearing on questions arising under those provisions, the Board has reason to believe that the aims of this Convention are being seriously endangered by reason of the failure of any country or territory to carry out the provisions of the Convention, the Board shall have the right to ask for explanations from the Government of the country or territory in question. Subject to the right of the Board to call the attention of the Parties,

the Council and the Commission to the matter referred to in sub-paragraph (c) below, it shall treat as confidential a request for information or an explanation by a Government under this sub-paragraph.

b. After taking action under sub-paragraph (a) above, the Board, if satisfied that it is necessary to do so, may call upon the Government concerned to adopt such remedial measures as shall seem under the circumstances to be necessary for the execution of the provisions of this Convention.

c. If the Board finds that the Government concerned has failed to give satisfactory explanations when called upon to do so under sub-paragraph (a) above, or has failed to adopt remedial measures which it has been called upon to take under sub-paragraph (b) above, it may call the attention of the Parties, the Council, and the Commission to the matter.

Article 19. Estimates of Drug Requirements

1. The Parties shall furnish to the Board each year for each of their territories, in the manner and form prescribed by the board, estimates on forms supplied by it in respect of the following matters:

a. Quantities of drugs to be consumed for medical and scientific purposes;
b. Quantities of drugs to be utilized for the manufacture of other drugs, of preparation in Schedule III, and of substances not covered by the Convention;
c. Stocks of drugs to be held as of 31 December of the year to which the estimates relate; and
d. Quantities of drugs necessary for addition to special stocks. . . .

Article 21. Limitation of Manufacture and Importation

1. The total of the quantities of each drug manufactured and imported by any country or territory in any one year shall not exceed the sum of the following:

a. The quantity consumed, within the limit of the relevant estimate, for medical and scientific purposes;
b. The quantity used, within the limit of the relevant estimate, for the manufacture of other drugs, of preparations in Schedule III, and of substances not covered by the Convention;
c. The quantity exported;
d. The quantity added to the stock for the purpose of bringing that stock up to the level specified in the relevant estimate; and
e. The quantity acquired within the limit of the relevant estimate for special purposes.

2. From the sum of the quantities specified in paragraph 1 there shall be deducted any quantity that had been seized and released for licit use, as well as any quantity taken from special stocks for the requirements of the civilian population. . . .

Article 24. Limitation on Production of Opium for International Trade

1. a. If any Party intends to initiate the production of opium or to increase existing production, it shall take account of the prevailing world need for opium in accordance with the estimates of thereof published by the Board so that the production of opium by such Party does not result in over-production of opium in the world.
b. A Party shall not permit the production of opium or increase the existing production thereof if in its opinion such production or increased production in its territory may result in illicit traffic in opium.

2. a. Subject to paragraph 1, where a Party which as of 1 January 1961 was not producing opium for export desires to export opium which it produces, in amounts not exceeding five tons annually, it shall notify the Board, furnishing with such notification information regarding:

    i. The controls in force as required by the Convention respecting the opium to be produced and exported; and

    ii. The name of the country or countries to which it expects to export such opium; and the Board may either approve such notification or may recommend to the Party that it not engage in the production of opium for export.

  b. Where a Party other than a Party referred to in paragraph 3 desires to produce opium for export in amounts exceeding five tons annually, it shall notify the Council, furnishing with such notification relevant information including:

    i. The estimated amounts to be produced for export;

    ii. The controls existing or proposed respecting the opium to be produced;

    iii. The name of the country or countries to which it expects to export such opium;

    and the Council shall either approve the notification or may recommend to the Party that it do not engage in the production of opium for export.

Article 28. Control of Cannabis

1. If a Party permits the cultivation of the cannabis plant for the production of cannabis or cannabis resin, it shall apply thereto the system of controls as provided in article 23 respecting the control of the opium poppy.

2. This Convention shall not apply to the cultivation of the cannabis plant exclusively for industrial purposes (fiber and seed) or horticultural purposes.

3. The Parties shall adopt such measures as may be necessary to prevent the misuse of, and illicit traffic in, the leaves of the cannabis plant.

Article 29. Manufacture

1. The Parties shall require that the manufacture of drugs be under license except where such manufacture is carried out by a State enterprise or State enterprises.

2. The Parties shall:
a. Control all persons and enterprises carrying on or engaged in the manufacture of drugs;
b. Control under license the establishments and premises in which such manufacture may take place; and
c. Require that the licensed manufacturers of drugs obtain periodical permits specifying the kinds and amounts of drugs which they shall be entitled to manufacture. A periodical permit, however, need not be required for preparations.

3. The Parties shall prevent the accumulation, in the possession of drug manufacturers, of quantities of drugs and poppy straw in excess of those required for the normal conduct of business, having regard to the prevailing market conditions.

Article 30. Trade and Distribution

1. a. The Parties shall require that the trade in and distribution of drugs be under license except where such trade or distribution is carried out by a State enterprise or State enterprises.
b. The Parties shall:
   i. Control all persons and enterprises carrying on or engaged in the trade in or distribution of drugs;
   ii. Control under license the establishments and premises in which such trade or distribution may take place. The requirement of licensing need not apply to preparations.
c. The provisions of sub-paragraphs (a) and (b) relating to

licensing need not apply to persons duly authorized to perform and while performing therapeutic or scientific functions.

2. The Parties shall also:

a. Prevent the accumulation in the possession of traders, distributors, State enterprises, or duly authorized persons referred to above, of quantities of drugs and poppy straw in excess of those required for the normal conduct of business, having regard to the prevailing market conditions; and

b. i. Require medical prescriptions for the supply or dispensing of drugs to individuals. This requirement need not apply to such drugs as individuals may lawfully obtain, use, dispense or administer in connexion with their duly authorized therapeutic functions; and

   ii. If the Parties deem these measures necessary or desirable, require that prescriptions for drugs in Schedule I should be written on official forms to be issued in the form of counterfoil books by the competent governmental authorities or by authorized professional associations.

3. It is desirable that Parties require that written or printed offers of drugs, advertisements of every kind or descriptive literature relating to drugs and used for commercial purposes, interior wrappings of packages containing drugs, and labels under which drugs are offered for sale indicate the international non-proprietary name communicated by the World Health Organization.

4. If a Party considers such measure necessary or desirable, it shall require that the inner package containing a drug or wrapping thereof shall bear a clearly visible double red band. The exterior wrapping of the package in which such drug is contained shall not bear a double red band.

5. A Party shall require that the label under which a drug is offered for sale show the exact drug content by weight or percentage. This requirement of label information need not apply to a drug dispensed to an individual on medical prescription.

6. The provisions of paragraphs 2 and 5 need not apply to the retail trade in or retail distribution of drugs in Schedule II.

Article 31. Special Provisions Relating to International Trade

1. The Parties shall not knowingly participate in the export of drugs to any country or territory except:
a. In accordance with the laws and regulations of that country or territory; and
b. Within the limits of the total of the estimates for that country or territory, as defined in paragraph 2 of article 19, with the addition of the amounts intended to be reexported.

2. The Parties shall exercise in free ports and zones the same supervision and control as in other parts of their territories, provided, however, that they may apply more drastic measures. . . .

Article 32. Special Provisions Concerning the Carriage of Drugs in First-aid Kits of Ships and Aircraft Engaged in International Traffic

1. The international carriage by ships or aircraft of such limited amounts of drugs as may be needed during their journey or voyage for first-aid purposes or emergency cases shall not be considered to be import, export, or passages through a country within the meaning of this Convention.

2. Appropriate safeguards shall be taken by the country of registry to prevent the improper use of the drugs re-

ferred to in paragraph 1 or their diversion for illicit purposes. The Commission, in consultation with the appropriate international organizations, shall recommend such safeguards.

3. Drugs carried by ships or aircraft in accordance with paragraph 1 shall be subject to the laws, regulations, permits and licenses of the country of registry, without prejudice to any rights of the competent local authorities to carry out checks, inspections, and other control measures on board ships or aircraft. The administration of such drugs in the case of emergency shall not be considered a violation of the requirements of article 30, paragraph 2 (b).

Article 33. Possession of Drugs

The Parties shall not permit the possession of drugs except under legal authority.

Article 35. Action Against the Illicit Traffic

Having due regard to their constitutional, legal and administrative systems, the Parties shall:
a. Make arrangements at the national level for coordination of preventive and repressive action against the illicit traffic; to this end they may usefully designate an appropriate agency responsible for such coordination;
b. Assist each other in the campaign against the illicit traffic in narcotic drugs;
c. Cooperate closely with each other and with the competent international organizations of which they are members with a view to maintaining a coordinated campaign against illicit traffic;
d. Ensure that international cooperation between the appropriate agencies be conducted in an expeditious manner; and

e. Ensure that where legal papers are transmitted internationally for the purposes of a prosecution, the transmittal be effected in an expeditious manner to the bodies designated by the Parties; this requirement shall be without prejudice to the right of a Party to require that legal papers be sent to it through the diplomatic channel.

Article 36. Penal Provisions

1. Subject to its constitutional limitations, each Party shall adopt such measure as will insure that cultivation, production, manufacture, extraction, preparation, possession, offering, offering for sale, distribution, purchase, sale, delivery on any terms whatsoever, brokerage, dispatch, dispatch in transit, transport, importation and exportation of drugs contrary to the provisions of this Convention, and any other action which in the opinion of such Party may be contrary to the provisions of this Convention, shall be punishable offenses when committed intentionally, and that serious offenses shall be liable to adequate punishment particularly by imprisonment or other penalties of deprivation of liberty.

Article 37. Seizure and Confiscation

Any drugs, substances and equipment used in or intended for the commission of any of the offenses, referred to in article 36, shall be liable to seizure and confiscation.

Article 38. Treatment of Drug Addicts

1. The Parties shall give special attention to the provision of facilities for the medical treatment, care, and rehabilitation of drug addicts.

2. If a Party has a serious problem of drug addiction and its economic resources permit, it is desirable that it estab-

lish adequate facilities for the effective treatment of drug addicts.

Article 39. Application of Stricter National Control Measures than those required by this convention

Notwithstanding anything contained in this Convention, a Party shall not be, or be deemed to be, precluded from adopting measures of control more strict or severe than those provided by this Convention.

THE FEDERAL STRATEGY FOR PREVENTION OF DRUG ABUSE AND DRUG TRAFFICKING

The Drug Abuse Policy Office issued this document from the White House in 1982.

The major elements of the federal government's strategy for reducing the availability of illicit drugs and reducing the adverse effects of drug abuse on the individual and society are:

International cooperation to interdict and eradicate illicit drugs, wherever cultivated, processed, or transported.

Drug law enforcement to reduce the availability of illicit drugs within the United States.

Education to discourage drug and alcohol use among youth under the age of eighteen, and to help parents recognize and deal with drug abuse in their homes, schools, and communities.

Prevention efforts to reduce the level of drug use among all Americans, especially school-age children, to encourage the provision of recreational and community-service activities as alternatives to drug use, to combat the problem of drunk driving, and to lessen the abuse of prescription and over-the counter drugs.

Detoxification and treatment services to be integrated into the general health-care system, and coordinated among private

industry, religious groups, private organizations, and state
agencies as support treatment programs.

Research to promote the production and dissemination of information about drugs, drug- and alcohol-use patterns, long-
term effects of drug usage, and the biological and psychological determinants of substance abuse; and to develop chemical
agents (agonists and antagonists) that will block or change the
expected physiological reaction to a drug.

Because drug and alcohol abuse by members of the armed forces
is a continuing concern, the Department of Defense has increased
its emphasis against the use of drugs and alcohol while on duty,
and has developed and refined drug monitoring and assessment
efforts, including urine testing for cannabis use.

GLOSSARY

Alcohol (ethyl alcohol). A depressant drug made by fermenting or distilling fruits, grains, or other foods.

Amotivational syndrome. An observed tendency in cannabis users to lose interest in purposeful activity.

Bootlegging. Smuggling or selling illegal alcohol to customers during Prohibition.

Cannabis (cannabis sativa). A fiber plant whose dried parts are used as a drug. Marijuana, hashish, and hashish oil are all derived from cannabis.

Chemical dependency. An inability to stop using a drug of any kind. Chemical dependency is a general term that today covers patterns of drug use that used to be called "habit," "addiction," etc.

Chemotherapy. The use of powerful chemicals (such as sulfanomides) to attack infection and cancerous growth.

Cocaine. A stimulant drug made by treating the leaves of the coca bush with various acids and other chemicals.

Controlled substance. Any drug the production and distribution of which is restricted by laws, such as the United Nations Single Convention on Narcotics Drugs, the Pure Food and Drug Act, or the Controlled Substances Act of 1970.

Crack. *See* **Free base**

DEA (Drug Enforcement Administration). The chief federal agency responsible for enforcing U.S. drug laws.

Decriminialization. An approach to drug laws that would lift criminal penalties for possession of small amounts of certain drugs, while maintaining laws against production and sale of drugs.

Depressant. A substance that slows down or blocks the performance of the nervous system.

Designer drugs. New mind-altering chemicals produced in laboratories.

Distillation. A means of producing highly concentrated alcohol by boiling fermented beverages, collecting the vapors, and then collecting the condensed vapors in liquid form.

Drug. A substance taken for the pleasurable feelings it produces.

EAP (Employee Assistance Program). A program adopted by organizations to help employees with drug problems.

Epidemic. A rapid increase of any phenomenon within a specific area.

Fatal dose. The amount of a drug that can kill a user.

Felony. A serious crime, carrying with it a possible jail sentence.

Free base. Purified cocaine made by treating the drug with a chemical solvent. The smoke from free-base cocaine is inhaled to produce the "high." Commonly called "crack."

Gas chromatography. A relatively elaborate, highly accurate form of drug testing.

Glaucoma. A disease that causes fluids within the eye to exert harmful pressure on other eye tissue.

Hallucinogen. A substance that distorts both the information coming into the brain and the brain's ability to interpret the information.

Medicine. A substance taken to relieve the symptoms of a disease.

Misdemeanor. A minor violation of the law, typically requiring the offender to pay a fine.

Prevention. An approach to drug abuse that, through education and public-health information, enables people to resist becoming involved with drugs.

Progressive disease. A disease, the symptoms of which, if not treated, will grow steadily worse until a person dies. Chemical dependency is regarded by many specialists as a progressive disease.

Prohibition. An approach to drug policy that aims at maintaining drug use at manageable and desirable levels.

Proof. An indication of alcohol content of a beverage. Proof equals twice the percentage of alcohol; that is, 40 percent alcohol equals 80 proof.

Psychoactive. Chemically able to alter the brain and, therefore, to alter states of mind.

Random screening. A system of drug testing in which certain members of an organization are selected at random and tested for possible drug use.

Recidivism. The tendency to return to a former pattern of behavior.

Remediation. The diagnosis and treatment of existing drug problems.

Sedatives. Depressant drugs prescribed as medicines to help people sleep or to relax.

Stimulant. A substance that excites the central nervous system to work harder and faster than it would normally.

Teetotalism. The practice of refraining altogether from alcohol.

Temperance. Moderate or restrained behavior. As an approach to alcohol, temperance means little or moderate use.

Testosterone. The male sex hormone most responsible for healthy sexual development and for the production of sperm cells.

THC (delta-9 tetrahydrocannabinol). The molecule in cannabis most responsible for making users high.

Threshold drug. A drug believed to lead to the use of other drugs.

Toxic. Contains toxins, or poisons. Toxic substances injure human cells and tissues.

Toxic dose. The amount of a drug that will make the user sick enough to require treatment.

BIBLIOGRAPHY

GENERAL STUDIES

Bejerot, N. *Addiction and Society*. Charles C. Thomas, Springfield, IL, 1970.

Carroll, C. *Drugs in Modern Society*. William C. Brown, Dubuque, IA, 1985.

Coles, R., and Kagan, J. *12 to 16 Early Adolescence*. Norton, New York, 1972.

DuPont, R. *Getting Tough on Gateway Drugs*. American Psychiatric Press, Washington, D.C., 1984.

DuPont, R.; Goldstein, A.; and O'Donnell, J. *Handbook on Drug Abuse*. U.S. Government Printing Office, Washington, D.C., 1979.

Erikson, E. *Childhood and Society*. Norton, New York, 1986.

————. *Identity: Youth, and Crisis*. Norton, New York, 1968.

Hawley, R. *The Purposes of Pleasure*. Independent School Press, White Plains, NY, 1983.

Johnston, L.; Bachman, J.; and O'Malley, P. *Drug Use Among American High School Students, College Students, and Other Young Adults*. National Institute on Drug Abuse, U.S. Dept. of Health and Human Services, Public Health Service, Alcohol, Drug Abuse, and Mental Health Administration, Rockville, MD, 1986.

Jones, H., and Jones, H. *Sensual Drugs*. Cambridge University Press, Cambridge, MA, 1977.

Julien, R. *A Primer of Drug Action*. Freeman, New York, 1978.

Lingeman, R. *Drugs from A to Z*. McGraw Hill, New York, 1974.

Macdonald, D., *Drugs, Drinking, and Adolescents*. Year Book Medical Publishers, New York, 1984.

Nahas, G., and Frick, H., eds. *Drug Abuse in the Modern World*. Pergamon Press, Elmsford, NY, 1981.

Richmond, J. *The Health Consequences of Smoking.* Report to the Surgeon General. U.S. Government Printing Office, Washington, D.C., 1981.

Roszak, T. *The Making of a Counter-Culture.* Anchor, Land-over Hills, MD, 1969.

Wilson, C. W. M. *Adolescent Drug Dependence.* Pergamon Press, Elmsford, NY, 1968.

SPECIAL TOPICS

Alcoholics Anonymous. *Alcoholics Anonymous.* Alcoholics Anonymous World Services, 1976.

Berry, F., and Boland, J. *The Economic Cost of Alcohol Abuse.* Free Press, New York, 1977.

Braude, M., and Szara, S., eds. *The Pharmacology of Marijuana Use.* Vols. I and II. Raven Press, New York, 1976.

Brewin, R., and Hughes, R. *The Tranquilizing of America.* Warner Books, New York, 1979.

Ellinwood, E., and Kilbey, M., eds. *Cocaine and Other Stimulants.* Plenum Press, New York, 1977.

Inhelder, B., and Piaget, J. *The Growth of Logical Thinking.* Basic Books, New York, 1958.

Jones, H., and Lovinger, P. *The Marijuana Question.* Dodd, Mead, New York, 1985.

Manatt (Schuchard), M. *Parents, Peers, and Pot.* National Institute on Drug Abuse, U.S. Dept. of Health, Education, and Welfare, Public Health Service, Alcohol, Drug Abuse, and Mental Health Administration, Prevention Branch, Division of Resource Development, Rockville, MD, 1979.

Nahas, G. *The Deceptive Weed.* Raven Press, New York, 1973.

———. *Keep Off the Grass,* 4th ed. Paul S. Eriksson, Middlebury, VT, 1985.

National Institute on Alcohol Abuse and Alcoholism. *Alcohol and Health.* U.S. Government Printing Office, Washington, D.C., 1981.

National Institute on Drug Abuse. _Opiates_, 3. U.S. Government Printing Office, Washington, D.C., 1983.

Peterson, R. _Marijuana and Health_. National Institute on Drug Abuse, U.S. Dept. of Health and Human Services, Public Health Service, Alcohol, Drug Abuse, and Mental Health Administration, Rockville, MD, 1980.

Rosenthal, F. _The Herb Hashish Versus Medieval Muslim Society_. Brill, 1971.

Russell, G. _Marijuana Today_. Myrin Institute for Adult Education, New York, 1980.

Turner, C., and Waller, C., eds. _Marijuana: An Annotated Bibliography_. Macmillan, New York, 1976.

U.S. Congress Subcommittee of the Committee on the Judiciary. _Marijuana-Hashish Epidemic and Its Impact on United States Security_. U.S. Government Printing Office, Washington, D.C., 1974.

U.S. Subcommittee on Criminal Justice. _Health Consequences of Marijuana Use_. U.S. Government Printing Office, Washington, D.C., 1980.

The American Council For Drug Education (ACDE), 5820 Hubbard Drive, Rockville, MD 20852, has published a series of monographs on current drug issues, including:

Blasinski, M., and Russell, G., eds. _Urine Testing for Marijuana Use_.

Cohen, S. _Cocaine Today_.

_____. _Cocaine Today: The Bottom Line_. and, Lessin, P. _Marijuana and Alcohol_ and, Andrysiak, T. _Therapeutic Potential of Marijuana's Components_.

Cook, P. _Drugs and Pregnancy: It's Not Worth the Risk_.

Dogoloff, L. _Urine Testing in the Workplace_.

Heath, R. _Marijuana and the Brain_.

Lantner, I. _A Pediatrician's View of Marijuana_.

Moskowitz, H., and Petersen, R. _Marijuana and Driving_.

Petersen, R.; Cohen, S.; Jeri, F.; Smith, D.; and Dogoloff, L. *Cocaine: A Second Look.*

Russell, G. *Marijuana Today: A Compilation of Medical Findings for the Layman.*

de Silva, R.; Dupont, P.; and Russell, G. *Treating the Marijuana-Dependent Person.*

Smith, C., and Asch, R. *Marijuana and Reproduction.*

Turner, C. *The Marijuana Controversy: Definition, Research, and Therapeutic Claims.*

Washton, A. *Cocaine Treatment: A Guide.*

ARTICLES

"Alcohol-Related Highway Fatalities Among Young Drivers: United States." *Morbidity and Mortality Weekly Report* 31: 641–44, 1982.

Anderson, K.; Cale, B.; Jackson, D.; et al. "Crashing on Cocaine." *Time*, April 11, 1983.

Baker, N. C. "Tough Love: New Way to Help Teens in Trouble." *Parents*, July 1977.

Bromwell, S. "How I Got My Daughter to Stop Smoking Pot." *Good Housekeeping*, March 1979.

Byck, R., and Van Dyke, C. "What Are the Effects of Cocaine on Man?" *Cocaine, 1977.* The National Institute on Drug Abuse, Washington, D.C., 1977.

Cutaia, J. H. "For Drug Makers, These Will Be the Good Ole Days." *Business Week*, January 12, 1987, 94.

Donovan, S., and Jessor, J. "Problem Drinking Among Adolescents: A Social-Psychological Study of a National Sample." National Institute on Alcohol Abuse and Alcoholism, Washington, D.C., 1976.

Edmundson, H. "Pathology of Alcoholism." *American Journal of Clinical Pathology* 74: 725–42, 1980.

Heath, R.; Fitzjarrell, A.; Fontana, C.; et al. "Cannabis Sativa: Effects on Brain Function and Ultra-structure in Rhesus Monkeys." *Biological Psychiatry* 15: 657–90, 1980.

"Is U.S. Becoming a Drug-Ridden Society?" *U.S. News and World Report,* August 7, 1978.

Jessor, R.; Chase, J.; and Donovon, G. "Psychosocial Correlates of Marijuana Use and Problem Drinking in a National Sample of Adolescents." *American Journal of Public Health* 70: 604–13, 1980.

Jessor, R., and Jessor, S. "Adolescent Development and the Onset of Drinking." *Journal of Alcohol Studies* 36: 27–51, 1975.

Jones, H. "What Practicing Physicians Should Know About Marijuana." *Private Practice,* January 1976.

Kitch, C. "On the Job Drug Tests: What to Know." *Good Housekeeping,* January 1987, 145.

Kolonsky, H., and Moore, W. "Effects of Marijuana on Adolescents and Young Adults." *JAMA* 216, 1971.

Lindsey, R., and Harmetz, A. "Hollywood's Drug Use Reportedly at 'Epidemic' Level." *New York Times,* November 2, 1982.

Phalon, R. "Sobering Facts on Rehabilitation." *Forbes,* March 9, 1987, 140.

Rubinow, D., and Cancro, R. "The Bad Trip: An Epidemiological Survey of Youthful Hallucinogen Use." *Journal of Youth and Adolescence* 6: 1–9, 1977.

Smith, W. "Drug Traffic Today: Challenge and Response." *Drug Enforcement* 9, no. 1, U.S. Department of Justice, 1982.

"This Is What You Thought: 56% Say Kids Should Report Drug Using Parents." *Glamour,* March 1987, 125.

Thomas, E., et al. "Drugs: The Enemy Within." *Time,* September 1986.

Warner, R., and Rosett, A. L. "The Effects of Drinking on Offspring." *Journal of Alcohol Studies* 36: 1395–1420, 1975.

INDEX

Abstinence from alcohol (teetotalism), 22, 23
Addiction (chemical dependency), 2, 51, 78
  alcohol, 5, 20–21, 26–27, 47–48, 59, 67, 69
  cocaine, 44–45, 47–48, 59, 67
  definition of, 2
  drug, 5–6, 44–45, 51–52, 59–67, 91
  heroin, 5, 67
  LSD, 67
  marijuana, 59, 67
  prescription medicine, 69
  programs to fight, 84–85
  tobacco, 5, 67
Advertising, liquor/tobacco industries and, 85
Age, legal. *See* Legal age for purchase of alcohol
Al-Anon, 101
Alateen, 101
Alcohol, 6, 12, 93
  addiction to, 5, 20–21, 26–27, 47–48, 67, 69
  and advertising, 85
  beer, 17, 18, 55, 56
  and the Bible, 17
  bootlegging of, 24
  brandy, 17
  in Canada, 56
  and crime, 24–26
  distilled spirits, 17
  and driving, 10, 12, 26, 47, 55, 56, 59, 67, 68, 74–75

and drug education, 12
effects of, 4–6, 12, 26, 47, 56–57, 59, 67–68, 90–91
in Egypt, 16
and European colonists, 18–20
fatal dosage, 56
gin, 17
history of, 16–27
and intoxication, 12, 18, 20, 22, 26, 56–58, 67, 68, 74, 87
and the *Koran*, 11, 17
legal age for, 55–59, 75, 78
lessons learned from easy availability of, 66–68
marijuana compared to, 29, 37
moonshining of, 25
in Moslem world, 11, 17
and Native Americans, 18–19
and organized crime, 25
and pregnancy, 26, 36–37
and Prohibition, 11–12, 24–25, 47
proof, 17, 65
rum, 17
and teetotalism, 23
and Temperance Movement, 20–22
tequila, 17
testing for, 71
use patterns of, 3, 25–26, 59, 65, 87, 93
vodka, 17
whiskey, 17, 18, 56
wine, 17, 18, 55, 56
Alcoholics Anonymous (AA), 2, 84–85, 101–3